Praise for *My Pe*

"Lucas' real-life account of his journey through and recovery from a mental health crisis is beautifully written and compelling. Countless young people who may be suffering will benefit from this inspirational story."

-Trish Larsen, Executive Director of Minding Your Mind

"I've read a lot of books on teen depression, anxiety, and suicide, and have never come across a book that can be so helpful for so many. Lucas' book will give HOPE to so many who struggle and will enlighten the many who love them and want to understand their struggle."

-Wendy Sefcik, Founder of RememberingTJ

"I know that Lucas' story will help society realize that the face of depression is not an obvious one. His story is raw and real, and indicative of so many youth today who struggle under the radar out of guilt and fear."

-De Snook, Co-founder of Warrior Families

"This book opened my eyes to the full, devastating power of depression and gave me an understanding I wouldn't think possible without experiencing it myself."

-Joe Wolfe, Lucas' twin brother

My Perfect Life

*How Depression Almost Ended It
And How I Found Purpose Through
Pain*

Lucas Wolfe

Dedication

To those struggling to find light in the darkness
That they may know the joy of hope, and comfort of relief.

"Never give in! Never, never, never.
In nothing, great or small, large or petty.
Never give in...
Never yield to force.
Never yield to the apparently overwhelming might
of the enemy."

-Winston Churchill

Why This Quote

Truth be told, to stand up to the illness is to go to war.
Along this path, many battles will be fought
Some ending in victory, some in defeat.
The force of the enemy is overwhelming
And in the shadow of its power,
We forget this eternal truth;
We are worth fighting for.
So never give in.
Never give in to depression!
Never give in to that dreaded demon of despair!
Never give in to the darkness!
Never, never, never.

While I strive for accuracy in this memoir, some names and characteristics have been changed to protect people's identity. There are also some events and conversations that have been compressed.

I am not a medical professional, and this book should not be used to replace treatment. Please always consult a trained professional before making any decisions regarding treatment of yourself or others.

Contents

Contents

Introduction:

My Perfect Life

I used to tell people I lived a perfect life. I grew up in a warm home with a loving family. I went to good schools and earned decent grades. I played a bunch of sports and had some talent at all of them. There wasn't anything I worried about. Not money. Not food. Not my future. I could do anything I wanted with my life. I could be anything I wanted. My life was perfect! But I wanted to die.

You're probably thinking that doesn't make any sense. Why would I want to die if I had such a great life? Yeah, I didn't have an answer for that either. I didn't know what was wrong with me. I only knew that something *was* wrong. But I never would have guessed it was depression. Not in a million years.

I used to think depression was mostly made up. Can you blame me? I mean seriously, we live in an age where people claim to be depressed because Kim Kardashian's second marriage only lasted 72 days! Who cares!? Nothing against the Kardashians, but I'd rather get punched in the face than watch their show. And don't even get me started on the people who think they have ADHD because they can't summon laser-like focus at will. Or the insomniac wannabes who never shut up about not falling asleep at the drop of a hat. That kind of narcissistic whining drove me nuts well before my battle with depression. There's a reason Millennials have a bad reputation; too many of us scream, "FEEL SORRY FOR ME" all the damn time. Apparently none of us learned the lesson from *The Boy Who Cried Wolf.*

Now, don't worry about this book railing against society and the "victim mentality" and all that nonsense. That's not what I'm here to do because that's easy, lazy, and achieves nothing. I only mention this stuff to establish some credibility with you. It's not lost on me that I come from a generation typically regarded as entitled, whiny, and lacking proper perspective. It's a bit of an unfair label that ignores the positive qualities of Millennials, but not altogether unwarranted. The point is, I understand you might not believe I struggled with depression. I mean, part of the title of this book is *My Perfect Life.* Why the hell would I be depressed? Good question.

Did something horrible or tragic happen to me to kickstart the depression? Nope. Did I have a rough childhood? Nope. Parents have a bitter divorce? No. They are still married after 30 plus years. Did I struggle with drugs? The law? Drinking? No, no, and not really. Did I suffer any type of abuse or relentless bullying? Nope. These are the usual suspects of depression. Even if someone has these "good" reasons for being depressed, we're often inclined to not totally believe them; without those reasons, well, what the hell is there to be depressed about?

I don't blame anybody or anything for this prevailing view towards depression; it's just the way it is right now. However, part of why I'm writing this book is to push back against that narrative. Before my experience with depression, I knew very little about the illness besides what I saw in commercials (cue the sad person staring out the window on a rainy day. Duh!). No one ever told me that depression can affect someone who lives a great life. I think that's because most people don't know it themselves. I obviously didn't know it. And it's not like depression just comes out of nowhere. A switch doesn't flip and all of a sudden – boom! – you're depressed. That's not how it happens.

Depression is a slow, creeping illness that slips over you as quietly as the night slips over the day. It's like trying to walk a narrow, winding path in the dark; even though you only take one step at a time, by sunrise you'll be a mile off the path without ever realizing it. Then you're hopelessly lost without the slightest clue of how to find your way back.

Much of the stigma surrounding depression stems from its abstract nature. Depression's typically thought of as a mood, like happiness, which implies we have a choice about it like the old adage attributed to Lincoln – "Folks are about as happy as they make up their minds to be." Well, depression is seen as the natural opposite of happiness, so Lincoln's saying could easily become, "Folks are about as depressed as they make up their minds to be." That's not totally true. Depression isn't a feeling; it's an illness.

And it isn't all that different from physical illnesses. Sometimes, no matter how well you take care of yourself, you still get sick. Nobody would think there's something fundamentally wrong with your character because you got the flu. We shouldn't think of depression or anxiety any differently. Depression is commonly shown to be the result of a chemical imbalance in the brain. I don't know about you, but I don't remember ever consciously balancing the chemicals in my brain. If you can do that, you should probably look into finding Charles Xavier and joining his school of X-men.

That being said, we do have control over how we think, which indirectly affects our brain chemistry. We can train ourselves to deal with stress, so we don't have as many negative, stress-related chemicals floating around in our brain. We can eat good food to ensure our body has the nutrients it needs. We can regulate our sleep, exercise, and treat ourselves well. All of these things have an effect on brain chemistry and can contribute to the development – or treatment – of depression.

Anyway, at the risk of putting the cart before the horse, let's get back to my previous analogy of walking off the path without realizing. That's how my depression developed. It was subtle and hazy, like a shadow in the dark. For years I knew something was happening to me, something that didn't feel right, but I didn't know how to explain it. I constantly reminded myself that my life was very blessed. I was easily happy. I had every reason to be happy. My parents are great parents. They always put us first (by us I mean me, my twin brother, Joe, and younger brother, Gabriel). My parents didn't have an easy childhood, and their adult lives haven't been a stroll in the park either. Joe and I were born 2 months early spending the first few weeks of our lives in the NIC unit for preemies. After us, my parents had Gabriel who was born healthy but contracted pneumococcal meningitis at 11 months old. The illness almost killed him, but Gabriel fought it and pulled through. Unfortunately, that battle for his life didn't leave him without scars; he is physically and mentally challenged. He can't talk or hear, and he has virtually zero independence. Despite all the difficulties he faced, and the enormous strain those difficulties put on my parents, they still managed to provide us with a beautiful life.

But as I got older, there were times when I felt off, like I was disconnected from the world around me – a spectator watching my life instead of an actor participating in it. I don't know why this happened. *Everyone feels alone sometimes* I'd tell myself. *What you're feeling is normal. It's normal, don't worry. You're fine.*

These minor interactions with the infant of despair first occurred in my junior year of high school. Everyone said adolescence was a weird time because of all the rapid changes taking place in our bodies at that age. I chalked those feelings up to side-effects of being a teenager and tried not to think about it past that. Fast forward to my senior year of college and I was standing on a metaphorical cliff begging God to push me off so I didn't have to jump myself.

It's a long way to fall from a happy teen to a suicidal college-student, but somehow, I managed to fall that far. Lots of people do, more and more these days. We've all seen these kinds of stories in the news. Smart girl or guy, funny, athletic, good looking. Beautiful personality. They have a great family and plenty of close friends. Most end up at a good college, some on a scholarship. Then one day they take their lives so suddenly it shatters the lives of everyone they knew. Loved ones are left to pick up the pieces, weaving together a picture that's only clear in hindsight; a beautiful soul desperately in pain, tortured by despair, eventually succumbs to their inner demons.

I never thought it could happen to me (we never do think the stories on the news can happen to us, do we?), but it did. I know what it's like to go from a happy, young guy to wanting so desperately to die I'd be willing to bring death about by my own hand. I know the sadness, guilt, confusion, dread, and brokenness that are all a part of depression. But much more importantly, I know the hope of recovery and the gift of a second chance at life.

That's why I'm sharing my story; I want you to know what I didn't – that others have felt this pain and chose life. You can choose life too. There's nothing you can't come back from. It feels impossible, and I thought it was impossible. When I finally reached out for help, I spoke with people who suffered from depression before me. These people are happy. They live good, full lives, and I never would've guessed they struggled with depression. When I told them how I felt, I could hear the pain in their voices as they pleaded with me to just hold on because everything passes in time. Their agony in hearing about my pain was so authentic, there wasn't a doubt in my mind they knew exactly how I felt. And here they were in front of me, happy, alive. It gave me hope.

Before I got help, I thought I was the only one in the world that ever felt the way I did. That probably sounds ridiculous since I just mentioned we've all heard these kinds of stories on the news, but depression does that to you. It warps your mind and blurs the line between reality and fiction like a vivid dream or, more accurately, like a nightmare. But knowing I wasn't alone, that was everything.

When I talk about depression, I often say I wish the person I am now, with the knowledge and experience I've gained, could go back and talk to younger-me. I'd tell him it was going to be ok, that he'd get through this. I'd tell him I'm sorry, so sorry, for the pain he's in, that it's not his fault, there's nothing wrong with him, and better days are ahead. I'd tell him there's help he can't even imagine. There's medicine and doctors and all kinds of things that aren't voodoo crap; they're life-saving miracles. I'd tell him there's a light at the end of the tunnel even if he can't see it, and even if he doesn't believe it. I'd tell him there's peace after pain, hope after despair, and a beautiful life on the other side of depression. I'd tell him to please, choose life.

I can't go back and tell myself those things. That's not how life works. But I can tell you. I can show you what I've learned so you don't carry the weight of depression for years and years like I did. So you don't think you're crazy or ungrateful or worthless. So you can recognize the signs in yourself, or a friend, or a loved one and get help before things spiral out of control. I can show you that no matter what you're going through, or what you might go through, there's always a way back to a fulfilling, joyful life.

And honestly, my descent into madness and subsequent recovery is pretty damn entertaining. I might be a bit biased about that, but I guess you'll just have to keep reading and see for yourself. What lies ahead are a series of stories that illustrate the creeping evolution of my depression, my battle against suicide, the realization that I needed help, and most importantly, how I found purpose through pain.

Part I – Depression and Recovery

The Beginning:

It Starts Small

It's hard to say exactly where my story starts, so I'll tell you about the first time I thought something might be wrong with me.

I was a junior in high school, and my Dad took Joe and I up to Penn State over the long, Labor Day weekend. The trip had the dual purpose of introducing us to the campus (we were beginning to think about what college to attend) and watching the Nittany Lions in person for the first time. I was pumped because I grew up listening to stories about Penn State. My Dad went there and graduated with a degree in mechanical engineering. Before him, his Dad, my Pop-Pop, went to Penn State for a year, then transferred to East Stroudsburg because he wanted to be closer to home. He had just returned from the Korean War, where he served as a paratrooper, and home helped him deal with post-war life. But he was always a Penn Stater at heart. When he grew old and Alzheimer's took most of him away, he still remembered Penn State.

I'll never forget the first time I laid eyes on the campus. It was a little after midnight and we cruised down College Ave in my Dad's 03' Chevy Impala like the homecoming chariot of a parade. "I Gotta Feeling" by the Black-Eyed Peas played on the radio. Packs of sun-kissed girls strutted across the streets. Guys greeted each other with a handshake-turned-one-armed-hug, the only acceptable way to say, "I missed you man." The air buzzed with excitement like a maddened hive of bees. Bits and pieces of a thousand conversations floated through the air gathering into the pleasant noise of an upbeat crowd. I was head over heels.

After checking into our hotel, we headed to the Diner, an iconic Penn State hotspot. Their specialty is the Sticky Bun which is basically a glazed cinnamon bun and yes, it's as delicious as it sounds. We sat in a glossy-red booth that looked like it belonged in a movie staged in the 50's. Joe and I listened to our Dad tell stories of his former glory days; stories we'd heard a thousand times but somehow never grew tired of. Maybe it's because my Dad lit up like a Christmas tree when he told these stories as if a great weight had been lifted from his shoulders. Maybe it's because they're funny as hell. Whatever it was, I always loved hearing those stories.

The next morning, we embarked on the long walk to Beaver Stadium, our sojourn to the Nittany Lions' Mecca. My Dad led us through campus pointing to buildings he took classes in commenting that most of them hadn't changed a bit since he was a student there. Hammond, a maze-like expanse of colorless brick that squatted on the edge of campus like a toad, was his favorite – or at least his favorite to talk about. There was a classroom on the second floor that had an inconspicuously broken door with a small dent in the bottom right-hand corner. My Dad said he and his roommates used to go there when they needed a quiet place to study because if you held the handle just right and kicked the dent in the door, it opened. Of course we took a detour on our way to the stadium to see if the old door trick still worked. It did.

As for the rest of the walk, well I had never seen so many people in my life! Beaver Stadium can hold upwards of 110,000 people, which transforms State College into the third most populous city in the state on gameday (behind Philly and Pittsburgh). Throngs of people decked out in navy blue and white drifted towards the stadium as if drawn by a magnet.

"You're gonna see a lot of that if you come here," my Dad said pointing to a family of Penn Staters. A middle-aged woman, her auburn hair pulled into a ponytail, smiled as her sons ran around her like a pack of puppies chasing their Mama. Her husband, wearing dark sunglasses and a navy jersey, held a toddler in his arms wearing the same outfit. "Lots of people meet here, get married, and raise a Penn State family. It's cool – it's just," my Dad paused for a minute, no doubt imagining us attending PSU and raising a Penn State family of our own. "It's just really something."

We made our way into the stadium about a half hour before kickoff. Our seats were in the nosebleeds, something I wasn't a fan of because high seats make me dizzy. But I was happy to watch the game on a beautiful Saturday afternoon, so I had nothing to complain about. It was my first college football experience, and I was impressed with what a spectacle it was. The Blue Band marched on the field with the synchronized precision of an army drill. Matt Freeman, the lead baton twirler, threw the baton so high I could've grabbed it from where I sat at the top of the stadium. He then proceeded to catch it between his legs after performing a cartwheel. Cheerleaders flipped through the endzone like trapeze artists accompanied by the jubilant cheers of the crowd. The iconic, Nittany Lion roar tore through the stadium bringing 100,000 roaring fans to their feet as the Penn State football team charged out of the tunnel. What an event! No wonder college football season is so beloved across the country. In that moment, I felt like I belonged at Penn State. Never had I experienced such an electric connection to a place!

Penn State played the Akron Zips that weekend and steam-rolled 'em. When we scored, the stadium erupted in a chorus of cheers, everybody high fiving everybody else. A chant for the wave got underway, and the student section kicked it off a moment later. Tens of thousands of arms rose and fell in unison, whipping their way across the stadium accompanied by more cheers from the crowd. It was about as perfect an afternoon as you could ask for.

After halftime, we went to get some food because the lines die down. Joe and my Dad stood in line, but I walked to the edge of the stadium to see if I could find my Dad's old dorm, Snyder Hall. I leaned against the concourse railing taking in the beauty of Happy Valley. The Appalachian Mountains – really nothing more than rolling hills – rose and fell against the horizon like a pod of dolphins leaping in and out of the ocean. A cool wind blew, a hint of autumn in its chill. RVs sprouted across the parking lot as if planted like rows of a farmer's crop. Tailgaters blossomed in the grassy areas beyond celebrating the arrival of a new football season like tulips celebrating the arrival of spring. And just beyond the tailgaters, a group of buildings rose out of the ground like a pack of mushrooms in an otherwise unblemished yard. The first of these buildings was Snyder Hall. I smiled when I saw it.

There was something surreal about looking at the dorm my Dad lived in knowing that many years ago he could have stood in the same spot taking in the same view. *Maybe I can come here too. Follow in my family's footsteps. Make them proud.* Because I wanted to make my parents proud, and I wanted to be proud of myself. I was a good student, and a decent kid, but I also had a streak of jackass in me. More often than not, my head was a swollen hot air balloon. I had a big heart, but an ego to match it. I think most of my friends would agree that I was a good friend to have, but if you called me an ass, I doubt they'd disagree. But my cockiness wasn't what bothered me most about myself. It was my deliberate laziness. My failure to give a hundred percent. My unwillingness to stretch for my full potential. That intentional lack of effort was wrong, and I knew it, but I refused to change.

Now, I think that's pretty normal for a high schooler to be honest. My Dad told me all the time that he was lazy and aimless up until his junior year of college. Faced with failing grades and a plummeting GPA, he arrived at a fork in the road. Drop out, or buckle down and resolve to succeed no matter the cost. He succeeded, but at the price of a lot of avoidable pain. Though he never actually said it, I think one of my Dad's missions in life was to make sure Joe and I never had to pay that same price.

I didn't want to ignore his advice anymore. I wanted to be better and to do justice to the life my parents gave me. They didn't put this pressure on me – I put it to myself. As I continued gazing across Happy Valley, my mind wandered to what my life could look like if I reached for my full potential. I didn't see the wild success of a lottery winner – there were no sports cars, or mansions, or designer clothing. I saw myself grounded like a sturdy oak. I was sure of myself. Mature, but not aloof. Firm, but compassionate. Knowledgeable, but not pretentious. Gone was the cockiness of adolescence and the laziness of youth. I saw myself growing up, becoming a man. The best part was how proud successful-me had made my parents.

Standing against the railing of the stadium, the warmth of contentment spread through my veins like a drug. *What a life I've been given. I'll make something of it, I will. I promise.*

Then I looked down.

The warmth drained out of me as if a demon lurked nearby. Icy tendrils tore their way through every nerve in my body.

Dread swallowed me like a wave crashing over my head as I gripped the railing for balance, my eyes transfixed by the inviting concrete a few stories below. I wanted to jump.

Two seconds. Two seconds, and it'll all just be over.

What...? What will be over? My life... why, why would you want that?

I didn't know. I didn't know why I wanted to jump. All I knew was I *did* want it. This wasn't the fleeting curiosity people experience when they are near the edge of a high place. No, this was wild-eyed craziness like George Bailey staring into the frigid river on Christmas Eve. The edges of my vision blurred until I could only see the concrete. My mouth became dry as sand. Dread gave way to euphoria. The fall would be quick. No pain. Then it would be over.

"Lucas," Joe yelled from a few feet away, his hands full with chicken tenders and Gatorade. "What're you doing? C'mon, we're gonna miss the game." Just like that I turned from the railing as if stepping out of a dream. We made our way back to our seats in time to see Penn State score again. On cue, I high fived those around me as if I hadn't just thought about throwing myself from the top of the stadium.

I didn't tell anyone what happened that day. How do you tell someone about those kinds of feelings? How do you tell someone you recognize you live a great life, a perfect life, but there's a part of you that doesn't want to live? And you don't even know why. People would think I was crazy! *I* thought I was crazy.

I never thought of this experience as a sign of functioning depression. I didn't even know functioning depression was a thing, but now I do. I recognize I tried to block out depression by always being "on." I moved from one activity to the next, never letting my mind rest, and talking a mile-a-minute to anyone who'd listen. I had a boundless supply of energy and bragged that sleep was for the dead. Even when I appeared to be doing nothing, my mind whirred at a dizzying pace like a demented merry-go-round. I despised silence and found darkness unnerving (I still slept with a night light in high school... yeah, that's embarrassing. Whatever).

Depression feels like losing your mind, especially in the beginning stages when it's not obvious you're depressed. The illness is portrayed as something akin to sadness, and that's definitely a component of it, but at the start, it's more like going mad. I didn't know that. I didn't know anything about depression. I thought it only affected people living through tragedy. I had no clue you could live a great life while depression grew in the recesses of your mind like a tumor. So, I tried to reason it away.

You're a teenager. Teenagers feel weird shit. Everybody says so. That's all it was.

Yeah. Yeah you're right. No big deal.

No big deal at all. Probably just stress, you know?

Definitely. I'm at this college – I have no idea what I want to study. No idea what I want to do with my life. That's stressful as hell.

Yeah, once I figure that out, I'll be good.

Sounded reasonable to me then, still sounds pretty reasonable now. I didn't have a clue what I wanted to do with my life, but it seemed like everybody else knew exactly where they were headed. Everybody walked along a well-worn path, but I was lost as shit. Nobody else wanted to jump from the top of a stadium, and that's because they were on their path. Once I got on my path, I'd be good.

With that naïve idea in mind, I went about the rest of my high school career doing what high schoolers do: complaining I had to learn the Pythagorean theorem because when am I ever going to use that in real life (never), worrying if the girl I wanted to ask to prom would say yes (she didn't), trying to decide what I'd study in college (no idea), and wondering what forbidden stuff I could get away with behind my parent's back. I was just a kid with a great life, a perfect life, and for 99% of the time I loved it.

That 1% though…

That 1% grew into 10% which grew into 50% and finally it just took over everything. Like most bad things, it started small, then snowballed out of control. There was always something over the horizon that would make it all better; a goal to be achieved, a mission to be accomplished, and then everything would fall into place (clearly, that's not what happened since I'm writing this book). So, I never said anything, never reached out for help. Who would believe me? My life was so perfect, what did I have to be depressed about? Besides, anytime I tried to explain what was happening, even to myself, it all sounded so normal. Yet, in my gut, I knew there was nothing normal about it.

Sophomore Year:

Failure and Change

Sophomore year was challenging. The novelty of college wears off a bit, and the focus shifts from meeting new people and making friends, to charting a path through life (because declaring a major is the know-all, end-all, right? It felt that way to me at least). Maybe the reason it felt like such a big decision was because I really didn't know what I wanted to do. I just kind of always did whatever was right in front of me, you know? Whatever I was *supposed* to do: Good grades? Check. Extra-curriculars? Check. Summer job? Check. Those were the right steps, and the path forward was clear, even if I didn't understand why I walked it. That changed when I went to college. Good grades were still part of the equation, part of what I was supposed to do, but what I wanted to do – well, I had no idea.

Have you ever seen the movie *Good Will Hunting*? It's a great movie; lots of life-lessons are packed into that film, and it's not told through a load of sappy bullcrap either. The main character, Will, is a veritable Einstein. Will's so gifted he makes the super-geniuses at MIT look dumber than Patrick Star, but he comes from a troubled part of Boston and frequently gets mixed up with the law. Eventually he gets in trouble one time too many and is about to be carted off to jail when, through a series of events, he accepts a plea deal to work with a college professor at MIT solving complex mathematical theorems. The catch? He's required to see a therapist.

Shockingly, Will isn't thrilled by the idea of seeing a therapist, but it's better than jail so he agrees. Will's a fast-talking loose cannon who does a better job analyzing the shrinks he's forced to see than they do of analyzing him. That is until he meets his match in a former MIT math-whiz-turned-psychologist named Sean. Sean earns Will's respect through some really fascinating interactions between the two, during which he frequently calls Will on his bullshit.

One of my favorite scenes in the movie occurs when Sean asks, "What do you wanna do?" and Will can't give a straight answer.

"You can do anything you want. You are bound by nothing," Sean says. "What are you passionate about? What do you want? I mean, there are guys who work their entire life laying brick so their kids have a chance at the opportunities you have here."

"I didn't ask for this," Will answers.

"No. You were born with it so don't cop out behind 'I didn't ask for this.' What do you really wanna do?" A long pause ensues, and you see the gears in Will's mind spinning as he tries to come up with a bogus answer just to be a jackass.

"I wanna be a shepherd. I wanna move up to Nashua, get a nice little spread, get some sheep and tend to them."

Sean's done with the crap. He tries chucking Will out of the office well before their session is over, but Will belligerently calls him out. He's adamant that Sean simply retired from the game of life after his wife died three years earlier and bashes him for it. For a moment, it looks like Will actually has the upper hand, like maybe Sean was a bit hypocritical.

"Look at me," Sean fires back. "What do you wanna do?" Will stares at him dumbfounded like a deer in headlights. "You and your bullshit," Sean continues. "You got a bullshit answer for everybody. But I ask you a very simple question, and you can't give me a straight answer. Because you don't know."

Boom! Sean 1, Will 0.

At the beginning of my sophomore year, I was lost just like Will. I took a bunch of AP classes in high school, got good SAT scores, ran varsity cross-country and track, got into a good college, took a ton of credits in various subjects, and got good grades in all of them. But I didn't have a damn clue why I was doing any of it.

Is that something to complain about? Oh, poor little me, right? I had such a good life, so much opportunity, I just didn't know what the *purpose* was. What a hardship!

I knew I had nothing to complain about, I didn't want to sound whiny, and I really didn't know how to articulate my confusion. Sean said, "I ask you a simple question" referring to "what do you wanna do?" but that didn't seem like a simple question at all. How can we possibly know what we're supposed to do with our lives? How do we know if we're reaching our potential, or if we're settling because it's easier? Where do we draw the line to say, "This is my best effort" versus "I can do more"? How do we know if we're making the right decisions? How can we ever know if we don't know the future? And how do we not obsess over making an irreversible life mistake? What the *hell* did Sean mean by "simple question"?

I used to be the guy with all the answers. Stress? That was for other people, not me. For a while that was true, and when it wasn't, I kept up the act. Life's a good time, and I was just along for the ride. Confusion, stress, failure, uncertainty; those emotions were the antithesis of how I defined myself. But sophomore year, I was totally confused, stressed to the max, failed at everything, and had no idea what I was doing. The seeds of depression were planted years before; now the climate was ripe for them to grow and thrive.

The "Freshman Year Recap" Story

The famous America poet, Maya Angelou, once said, "You can't really know where you're going until you know where you've been." I figured I'd take her advice and tell you about my freshman year, so you understand the rest of my college experience.

That first year was totally awesome. I wasn't nervous the way most people were. Joe and I roomed together (interestingly, we lived in Snyder Hall, the same dorm our Dad lived in), so I didn't have to worry about getting a roommate from hell. As for making friends – well, I could talk to anybody about anything because I loved talking. In a school of over forty thousand people, the odds were in my favor that I'd find at least a few that liked me. Besides, everybody was in the same boat; no one knew each other, and no one wanted to be left out. We all got a fresh start, a clean slate. It's easy to meet people when you're on an equal playing field.

And speaking of meeting people, on August 20, 2011, the day after I moved into the dorms, I met Erica. We talked a few times through an incoming freshman Facebook group where people shopped around for a roommate. I didn't need a roommate, but I figured I might as well talk to people in my class and make some friends before school started. When dorm assignments got sent out in July, Erica and I discovered we were slated to live in the same building and agreed to meet up at school. None of our conversations amounted to more than small talk, so I didn't think anything of it.

When I knocked on her door, Snyder 203, she answered with a bubbly smile that made her eyes squint. That's all it took;

I was hooked. I'm not a romantic, and lovey-dovey clichés make me want to barf, so it irritated me how much I liked this girl right away for no reason. Her twin brother, who was also in the room, seemed wholly uninterested in introducing himself. He wore a shirt with a picture of a chick and a magnet with the words "Chick Magnet" predictably written beneath. *What a douchebag.*

A few days later, Erica came to my room and asked if I believed in love at first sight. If Joe wasn't studying at his desk 3 feet away from us, I would have said, "You felt that too?" (or at least I'd like to think I would have had the balls to say that). Instead I gave a nondescript answer. But Erica and I both knew why she asked that question, and soon after we began dating.

As far as my classes went, they were harder than anything I'd taken in high school, but I also tried harder than in high school. My Dad told me for a long time that freshman year of college would be the easiest, and to make sure I got good grades as a buffer for later years. Great advice; it's the only reason I managed to graduate with a decent GPA (I entered freshman year with an undecided major but took classes as if I leaned engineering).

The weeks ticked by at a blistering pace and I was always "on." I loved it! My workload was insane, but it didn't overwhelm me. I made friends in my classes and at least half of my floor enrolled in engineering, so we often studied for exams and did homework together. After a difficult test, we'd head back to the dorms and play Beerio-Kart to unwind. I wasn't much of a partier in high school, so it surprised me how much I genuinely enjoyed drinking.

The frat parties were legendary, but that also meant they weren't easy to get into. You had to know somebody, and I was never good at the you-scratch-my-back-I-scratch-yours networking needed to get an "in." Fortunately, most frats had a terrible system of identifying people allowed into the party; a standard color wristband indicated you were on the list of entrants. Someone from Snyder bought about 1,000 wristbands off the internet, and every weekend, we'd use them to sneak our way into parties. It made taking candy from a baby look difficult, and the frats didn't catch on until late in the year. Then they ordered custom-made wristbands that were nearly impossible to duplicate. Oh well. It was fun while it lasted.

So yeah, everything about freshman year was awesome. I met a ton of new people, made hilarious memories, fell in love, partied hard and worked harder. My friends and I often say we'd trade 5 years at the end of our lives for a chance to relive our freshman year. And why not? It was perfect... until the very end (dun, dun, dun!).

About a week before the end of spring semester, it dawned on me that I'd have to declare a major in the fall. That didn't give me much time. I'd been thinking about what I wanted to do for years; now I only had a few months, and I was no closer to deciding. I kept coming back to engineering, but as much as it interested me, it only felt like what I was supposed to do – the next right step. That didn't necessarily mean I was meant to be an engineer, or that I even *wanted* to be one. But what I wanted didn't matter to me as much as taking the next right step. A college degree was the endgame of all these right steps, and not just any degree, but a good one. A degree that paid the bills. A degree that afforded opportunity. A degree that gave me the freedom to build whatever type of future I wanted for my life. But I couldn't see a future for myself.

Struggling to declare a major, to chart a path through life, that felt normal to me. Lots of people struggle with these decisions. But not being able to see a future? That felt off, like a word on the tip of my tongue that I never remembered. It scared me. When you're young, you can always see yourself in the future. You see yourself being able to drive, growing up and becoming a cop or a doctor or an astronaut, having a family and a home and maybe a dog or two. When you're in middle school, you see yourself in high school. When you're in high school, you see yourself in college. When you're in college, you see yourself in the real world. And I'm not talking about this in the sense of you can't enjoy the present moment; I just mean, even if we are enjoying the present moment, we're always looking ahead. I've always been able to see that next step, but at the end of freshman year, I couldn't. There was just blackness.

I made a point of spending time by myself – a half hour here or there at a quiet spot on campus – to think about what I wanted for my life. I figured a little introspection might be useful, however these moments of self-reflection didn't last long. They always brought on feelings of dread similar to what I experienced at the top of Beaver Stadium. An overwhelming sense of doom engulfed me as if I were trapped at the bottom of a well filling with water. And if I suffered these depressive episodes a few days in a row, nightmares began to plague my sleep.

It occurred to me that this wasn't normal; something was wrong, but I didn't know how to explain it. Anytime I imagined talking about what I was going through, my "problem" sounded inconsequential like complaining about burning a finger on the stove while the Camp Fire torched half of California. I really believed my pain came from the uncertainty of my life moving forward – the product of too much opportunity rather than too little. But one way or another, my life would move forward, so why talk about how I felt? Why expose myself to that shame and humiliation? Why not just push forward and let things work themselves out?

The day before we went home for the summer, Erica broke up with me. I was crushed. And blindsided. There wasn't anything wrong between her and I, but her family hated me. It's hard to say why because they never met me, but all year they tried bullying Erica into ending it. In the end, they offered an ultimatum: dump Lucas or you don't go back to Penn State (I realize this sounds far-fetched like it can't possibly be the complete story, but it is. I've got no intention of dragging her family through the mud though; I only mention this stuff because Erica's resilience throughout our relationship plays a role in my recovery. Spoiler alert: her and I are married now).

That summer sucked. I enrolled in a physics course at a Penn State branch campus near home so I could declare a major in engineering in the fall. When I wasn't in class, I worked as a lifeguard. Not really the best job for someone who didn't like to turn "off." What I needed was a hard reset – something to wipe the slate clean. The start of sophomore year provided that reset. I had a lot of hope going into the fall semester. Hope that I'd declare the right major. Hope that I'd figure out my life. Hope that the depressive episodes would end once I got on the right path. But hope without action is a house of cards built on sand – it didn't take long for it to all come crashing down.

The "Choosing A Major" Story

What do you love to do? Have you figured that out yet? Maybe you like doing a lot of things and can't quite figure out which one you love doing? That was part of my problem. I liked math, chemistry, and biology. I liked to read and write and tell stories. I liked economics, politics, history, religion, and – well, you get it, I liked pretty much everything. How could I possibly decide on a major? What if I picked the wrong thing and screwed my life up? I didn't think I'd be able to live with myself if I did that.

I was handed a perfect life, but it didn't fall out of the sky like manna in the desert. My parents worked hard to give me that life. They didn't have it easy growing up, especially my Mom, and they didn't want their children facing the difficulties they did. So they sacrificed. They dedicated themselves to giving us a better life than they had. Their reward for all that hard work? A lazy, arrogant, immature, wise ass – me.

I doubt my parents would agree with that characterization; sure, I had elements of those qualities, but that certainly doesn't describe the whole person. Depression always magnifies the negative, tricking those who struggle with the illness into believing they're terrible people. I began to believe I was a terrible person as I finished high school. I hated myself for how lazy I was. I failed AP Math, AP Chem, and AP Comp Sci in my senior year simply because I didn't do any work. Nothing. And it's not like I didn't have the time. I just threw away opportunity because I was too stupid to realize what a gift it was.

The worst part? I went to a college-prep school; that's not free. My family isn't poor, but we're not filthy rich either. My parents made an *enormous* sacrifice sending us to private school. Now they were paying for college too. And I just... I just acted like I was entitled to all of it.

You're such a jackass.

I know.

You never did a thing to deserve any of this.

I know!

Think of everything they could've done with that money.

I KNOW!

And I did think about what they could've done with that money. They could have bought a shore house, or a mountain house, or maybe just a second house because they felt like it.

They could've gone on more vacations, traveled the world, or gone on private safaris. They could've bought a more luxurious car, or a bigger TV, or gone out to eat every single night so they never had to make dinner or clean dishes. Or they could have just saved it so they had a buttload for retirement. But they didn't. They spent it on me, and I didn't do a damn thing to deserve it.

What brought about this sudden revelation that should have been obvious my entire life? Going to college because Gabriel never would. Leaving home was a gut-punch comparison of our lives and the differences in our potential future. Gabriel's future consists of whatever others will give him; by himself, he has no future. He'll never go to college. He'll never have a job. He'll never raise a family. Technically, he'll never mature past the age of a 6-year-old. He can't talk, or hear, or read, or write, and his favorite show at 25 years old is Elmo. Yet, here I was, *bound by nothing*, and I wasted it because I was too busy being a damn clown. I refused to repeat that sin in college; I'd redeem myself.

It's with that mindset – an obsession to not waste my life and to make up for past mistakes – that I went about deciding a major. To be fully dramatic about it, I agonized over the decision (don't worry, I've already got the world's smallest violin out for myself). There are tons of people who will never have the opportunities I did, Gabriel being one of them. People growing up in the ghetto with a gang as the only family they've ever known. Kids going to school with empty bellies. Veterans, homeless and alone. Drug addicts stigmatized and forgotten. Children dying well before their time. Pain is all around us. Tragedy is common. There are millions – no, billions – billions of people with lives more difficult than mine. I knew that, yet no matter how much "perspective" I forced on myself, I couldn't shake my comparatively, non-existent problem. Anxiety, depression – they both convince you that you have no right to feel the way you do because you're not broke, homeless, and starving. They made me believe I hadn't earned the right to be depressed. My life was easy, and I had the world at my fingertips; who would believe me if I told them I was in pain? I didn't even believe myself.

I needed help, but a few years would pass before I understood that. Sometimes, we're not supposed to do it all ourselves. Sometimes it takes more strength to ask for help than it does to bear a burden alone. Cliché, I know. It used to tick me off when people parroted that absurdity. It's the same as saying, "It doesn't matter who wins or loses, as long as you had fun." Bullshit. Only losers say that. I thought the "it takes more strength to ask for help" nonsense was an excuse made by weaklings who couldn't handle life on their own. Turns out I was wrong.

Anyway, back to deciding a major. Part of me wanted to major in English because I loved writing and always dreamed of being an author (although never in a million years did I think this was the book I'd write). Another part of me wanted to dual major in politics and business; degrees that potentially opened the door to law school, a political career, or a financial-sector job. I was also intensely interested in biology and biochemistry. I found anatomy fascinating, especially at the cellular level where hundreds of molecules work in concert to carry out a cell's designated function (did you know that if you took all the DNA out of your cells and stretched them out, they'd be about twice the length of the Solar System?! The Solar System is 7.5 *billion* miles long! Mind = blown).

But I always circled back to chemical engineering. The idea of it was stuck in my head like that God-awful Kars-for-kids jingle. I couldn't really explain why. The subject of it appealed to me, but not more or less than anything else. Maybe I liked Chem E because it was broad; it contained a lot of crossover with other engineering and science disciplines. Maybe I liked that it gave me options down the road. If I decided I wanted to study law or go into politics, I could do that after earning an engineering degree. If I wanted to jump into the medical field, Chem E provided a solid scientific foundation for that career path too. And if I wanted to write a book then I could do that while working a job that paid the bills. But I think what mostly drew me to chemical engineering was that it was hard. Everyone I asked said it was really hard. Like, stupidly hard. *Good. That's what my lazy ass needs.* But I was far from certain that studying Chem E was the right move.

Was I only doing it out of guilt? My parents wanted me to work hard, but they didn't think I owed them for past mistakes. In fact, they'd tell you they were proud of what I accomplished in high school. Proud! Not disappointed. I put that on myself, and that's really why I struggled to declare a major. Depression made me feel unworthy. I didn't deserve my perfect life. I didn't deserve to go to college. I didn't deserve a good job. I didn't deserve success. I hadn't earned any of it, but if I picked the right major, I believed I could earn it. I'd redeem myself and prove I wasn't a waste.

I didn't feel resolve as I faced these character flaws. There was none of the excitement inherent in turning a corner; I only felt fear. What if I couldn't make it through this major? What if I totally failed and was exposed as a fraud and an idiot? What if I chose to study Chem E for the wrong reasons and still ended up wasting my life? What if I was supposed to do something else and one day found out that I made the wrong decision? What if, what if, what if…

Wrestling with these permutations of the future brought to mind *The Road Not Taken* by Robert Frost, a poem I learned as a freshman in high school. The first time I read it I thought it was dumb mostly because I didn't get it at all. Now, it began to make sense to me. It reads in part:

Two roads diverged in a yellow wood,
And sorry I could not travel both
And be one traveler, long I stood
And looked down one as far as I could
To where it bent in the undergrowth;

Yet knowing how way leads on to way,
I doubted if I should ever come back.

I shall be telling this with a sigh
Somewhere ages and ages hence

We all have been at a fork in the road where different, distinct paths lay in front of us. Maybe it was 2 paths or 4 paths or 100 paths. Doesn't matter. We see the implications of each path, each choice, but only for a short distance into the future – "to where it bent in the undergrowth." None of us can see past that; we don't get to know the consequences of our decisions ahead of time. We all need to take a leap of faith, and then find a way to live with our choices because we can't go back and make different ones. We may wonder what our lives would look like if we walked a different path. We may feel nostalgia for a version of our lives unlived, but we don't get to go back.

It's normal for us to wrestle with these decisions. What wasn't normal was my inability to let go and trust myself. Depression erodes the trust you have in your decisions. When you're having one of the best days of your life, and all of a sudden you *want* to throw yourself off the top of a stadium, you lose trust in yourself – and you avoid high places. When you think about your future and the same life or death dread envelops you, you avoid thinking about your future.

A war raged within me between my real-half and my depressed-half. I didn't know it was depression back then, but I knew a monster lived in me, like Bruce Banner living with the Hulk. Bruce is afraid to be around people. He's afraid to say what he really thinks. He's afraid to feel how he really feels, because at any moment the Hulk may come out and destroy everything. Bruce didn't trust himself because he didn't understand the monster that lived in him, and I didn't understand the depression living in me either. But I still had a choice to make at the end of fall semester; study chemical engineering despite my doubts, or find another path.

I chose chemical engineering.

Many times over the following months and years, I wanted desperately to switch out of Chem E, but I never pulled the trigger. I stayed in the major when I stopped liking it. I stayed when I hated it. I stayed when it was destroying me, and I knew it was destroying me. I stayed because something happened over the winter break before my first Chem E classes that convinced me I was *supposed* to study chemical engineering. I believed this sign proved my life wouldn't be wasted if I studied Chem E. That faith made the pain worth enduring.

So, I took the leap, and prayed I wouldn't smash into the rocks below.

The "First of Many Epic Fails" Story

I started my Chem E career in a class called Mass Balances. It's the first course Chem E's take, and you need to pass with a "C" or better to enroll in any other chemical engineering classes. The professor told us it was a tough class, but also the easiest Chem E class we'll ever take. "If by the end of this course, you don't score a 'C' or better, you should very seriously consider another major," he said. (I'll let you take a guess right now as to what grade I got. Hint: I seriously considered switching majors at the end of the semester).

Ninety percent of our grade was determined by seven quizzes, one every other week, while the remaining ten percent was determined by homework. Our lowest quiz grade would be dropped, excluding the final. That was the department's way of easing us into a core curriculum course; they gave us a mulligan.

"You should look ahead in the semester," my Dad said when I told him about the mulligan. "You've got a lot of hard classes with Thermo and Ochem and whatnot. Find the week you might be overloaded and let the Mass Balances quiz slide a little if you have to. You still want to try and do well, but it's always nice to have a bit of a buffer in there."

Good plan, great advice. Didn't quite work out that way.

The first quiz we took was easy. Everyone I asked said it was really easy. Like, stupidly easy. I got a 50.

What the hell!

Maybe I should've picked a different major.

Dude, it's one quiz.

Yeah, and I got a 50... that sucks ass.

And that's not even the worst part of this epic fail. No, the worst part was that I cheated and *still* got a 50! The quiz was supposed to be simple, but I couldn't remember a damn thing when it was put in front of me like I got blasted with the neuralyzer from *Men in Black*. It was a single question consisting of multiple parts 'a' through 'f.' You had to solve 'a' to get 'b,' 'b' to get 'c' and so on. Well, I had no idea how to solve 'a,' and didn't even know what the other parts were talking about.

Back then, I panicked about as much as Nick Fury (that guy didn't even blink when his partner turned to dust right in front of his eye. Ha! See what I did there?). But I panicked taking this quiz. I'm pretty sure my brain short-circuited because almost half the period went by, and I had nothing. If I didn't come up with an answer quick, I'd get a zero. So, I looked at the guy's paper next to me. Totally cheated off him. I was desperate; my entire life hung in the balance!

Duh! Dear God I knew I was dumb, but I didn't know I was that dumb!

To get the answer to 'a,' I simply had to rearrange a basic equation and solve for the remaining variable, something that should have taken me all of a minute to figure out. Unfortunately, the guy next to me finished his quiz early leaving me to solve the rest on my own. It didn't go well.

I couldn't believe it. I studied harder for that test than any other in my life and got demolished. If it only got more difficult from here on out, how would I ever make it through this major? Was I about to flush two years of paid-for college down the drain? This was supposed to be my time for redemption, my time to make up for past failures. Instead, I screwed myself! And I cheated!

And that's what really ticked me off. I was mad at my poor performance, but I was livid that I cheated. I hated cheaters! All through high school I watched people cheat, watched them lie and steal their way to a grade they didn't earn or a recognition they didn't deserve. That might have been tolerable if it weren't for the fact that these weasels puffed out their chests like pretentious peacocks as if they were gods among peasants. The hypocrisy of it made me want to throw up. Yet, when the chips were down and I was in the hot seat, I pulled the weasel move.

Now, did taking a quick peek at my neighbor's quiz really matter in the grand scheme of things? On one hand, no. On the other, of course it did! Cheating is wrong and I wanted to beat up on myself for doing it. Depression does that; it takes small mistakes and blows them up into life-ending calamities. Everything is life and death to someone fighting depression. To a healthy person, it's just one quiz for one class for a major I didn't have to take. It's a drop in the bucket. It's a minute out of a year, a day out of a lifetime. It's forgettable. But with depression, it's everything. It's the *only* thing.

I didn't understand that at the time because my depression was in its early stages. I didn't know how far I could fall, or that the mundane, routine occurrences of everyday life could render me bed ridden. I didn't understand that depression is intelligent. It's convincing, so much so that it persuades people into killing themselves to escape it. If you haven't felt the scourge of depression, let that statement sink in for a moment. People kill themselves to escape its agony. Many others consider suicide before they get help. I did.

But like I said, I wasn't there yet, so I forgave myself for cheating and vowed to never do it again. I committed myself to working even harder to do better on the next quiz, and the one after that, and all the rest of 'em. Redemption was still within sight; I refused to be discouraged.

Something in me was changing though, something fundamental. It made me uneasy like when it's too quiet in a horror film and you know something terrible is about to happen. I wondered if something terrible was about to happen to me.

The "Time I Was Too Scared to Play Basketball" Story

"Wow," I said as James shot another airball. "You really suck." Sumit, James, and I just finished working out, so our arms were pretty dead, but it was still embarrassing to shoot a bunch of airballs, so I gave him crap for it.

"I'd like to see you do better," James replied tossing me the ball.

"No problem. I'll put up a half court on the first try," I answered. James said something about there being no way in hell

I'd make that shot, I was too scrawny, I sucked at basketball, I was a jackass, blah blah blah. James could be a bit sensitive. I tuned him out. After talking a big game, it was time to step up.

I stood at half court looking bored and amused at the same time, like Usain Bolt about to run against a JV high schooler. Endorphins surged through my veins as I envisioned shooting a perfect swish. Time slowed and the world around me dissolved. There was only me, the ball, and the basket.

In one smooth motion I jumped into the air and launched the basketball in a high arc towards the net. The second it came off my fingertips, I knew it was good. "In," I declared walking off the court without watching as my shot landed a perfect swish. Sumit shook his head in disbelief while James muttered a string of curses to himself. I strutted off the court with the swagger of a gold-medal Olympian. Nothing made me happier than talking a big game and backing it up when the pressure was on.

Now I'll admit the stakes weren't high. It's not as if this was the buzzer-beater game-winning shot in the March Madness championship. I was just messing around with my roommates, but all the same, I relished the somewhat high-pressure situation. People tend to shrink away from the spotlight, but I jumped toward it every chance I got. I loved the opportunity to perform and bask in the glory of my own awesomeness afterwards. I loved the competition. I loved how it filled me with life, how the world melted away in a single climactic moment where I either stepped up, or I didn't.

Late in the spring semester, I sat against the wall of that same gym with Joe, Sumit, James and Luke waiting for our turn to get on the court. A group of guys had been on a long winning streak that we hoped to end. I couldn't wait to get out there and lose myself in the thick of competition. Everything would fade away except for this pick-up game, and I needed that because things weren't looking great at the moment.

After I got my first Mass Balances quiz back, I figured that'd be my mulligan. I got a 50; who wouldn't assume that'd be the mulligan? Well, my dumb ass got a 30 on the next quiz (at least I didn't cheat on that one), and another 50 on the one after that. A "C" looked increasingly impossible, like fighting Thanos after he had three Infinity stones, and we all know how that worked out before Iron Man saved everyone.

I was also failing Thermo, my other introductory Chem E course. I got a 52 on the midterm, but that was nothing more than a stroke of dumb luck. One of the exam questions was almost exactly the same as a question asked during the *one* office hours I attended. I still didn't understand it when I took the test, but I've got a solid memory, so I wrote what I remembered. Of the 52 points I scored on that exam, 23 of them came from that question. This only reinforced the idea that I was a fraud who'd end up wasting all the sacrifices people made to give me my perfect life.

Then there were the rejections from every internship I applied to. I can't really blame the companies that rejected me; my grades were abysmal. But it still stung, especially since Joe accepted a great internship with Lockheed Martin over the summer. I was happy for him. Joe deserved an internship more than anyone I knew, yet his success left me feeling untethered like a leaf aimlessly blowing in the wind after it falls from its tree. Joe and I are twins. We did everything together our entire lives, but not this summer. I had my failures to thank for that.

My love life hadn't improved either. Erica and I tried to stay away from each other in the beginning of the year, but we were both unhappy. Neither of us did a good job dealing with the breakup because we didn't accept it. We still wanted to be together, so we began dating again just before Christmas break, only this time it was in secret. If her twin brother found out we were together, he'd rat us out, and if that happened, Erica would get pulled out of Penn State. Not an ideal situation to say the least.

Towards the end of February, we went to a party together. A friend of ours from Snyder, who knew of our dilemma, hosted it, so we thought it'd be safe to attend. We thought wrong. My "friend" went and told Erica's brother we were together. To this day, I have no idea why, but I can tell you it didn't feel great getting stabbed in the back. Her brother went ballistic and threatened to kill me (a tiny bit of an overreaction in my opinion). The next day, I spent a couple hours on the phone with Erica's Mom convincing her to let Erica stay at Penn State. She agreed to back down, but only after I agreed to stay away from her daughter forever. Nothing like promising to stay away from the love of your life to lift your spirits a little.

A few days after that phone call, I had an Ochem exam. I got a 12. Yupp, a 12 out of 100. It would've been funny if it weren't so sad. You almost have to try to do that bad. Obviously, I dropped the course because there's no way to recover from a 12 (*that* was the worst failure I had in my college career).

As I sat against the wall waiting for my turn to get on the court, I questioned if every leap of faith was a great idea. Maybe sometimes it wasn't a leap of faith. Maybe sometimes it was just a stupid jump off a cliff. I took the leap into Chem E praying that I wouldn't hit the rocks below and I didn't. I smashed into them like a screaming comet. And I was angry about it. Angry that I felt misled to study Chem E. Angry about my failures in school and with Erica. Angry that these minor inconveniences could derail me so thoroughly that I felt as if I was falling apart.

What the hell is your problem, man?

I don't know.

You disgust me.

29

Me too.

Fuck you. It's a couple tests. Get over it.

You think I don't want to?

So shit went bad with Erica. Get over it. People have got it a hell-of-a-lot worse than you.

I know!

Then why're you feeling sorry for yourself?

I'm not feeling sorry for myself! I don't know what's wrong with me!

You're pathetic.

Fuck you.

"We're up," Luke said jarring me out of the battle between my depressed-half and real-half. I popped up off the floor and jogged onto the court. We shot for first ball even though winners generally kept, but we missed, and they kept anyway. This wouldn't be an easy game to win; they had a significant height advantage. The smallest guy on their team was about my height (I'm just shy of 6 feet – which really ticks me off by the way. Like c'mon I couldn't have grown one more quarter inch to round out at a nice even 6 feet?) and none of them appeared to suffer from white man's disease like I did. We'd have to play smart. That was the only way we'd beat them, but I knew we could do it. My roommates and I all had different talents we could draw from to frustrate their defense. Luke drove hard to the basket. Joe could pop shots with three people covering him. James made wild pivots under the boards to put up layups against much taller defenders. Sumit juked people out of their shoes. I shot the long ball. Together, our team had the talent, now it was only a matter of stepping up.

The other team drained a few buckets in the beginning and pulled ahead right away. I wasn't worried – it was early in the game – but I didn't feel good either. The competitive trance I loved hadn't taken over yet. I tried turning it on again and again, but like a sputtering engine that won't turn over, it gave out. I simply couldn't get in the zone.

"Lucas!" Joe yelled passing me the ball from the top of the key. I was wide open behind the three-point line a few steps from the corner of the court, a very low percentage shot, so one of my favorites. I lined up my shot but didn't feel the familiar adrenaline rush. Instead, doubt pushed its way into my mind like an unwelcome stranger. For a moment I froze, and the defense pounced forcing me to dump the ball back out to the top of the key.

What was that?

Eh, just got in my own head. I'll hit the next one.

Yeah hit the next one. Let's go. You got this.

But I didn't hit the next one. I didn't hit anything because I didn't take a shot all game. Depression blocked the usual rush of competition. It took me out of the game like I was an apparition watching this fear-stricken version of myself attempt to play. My legs carried me up and down the court, but I don't remember telling them to. I'd get the ball, dribble a few times, accomplish nothing, and pass it away. At every moment I expected to snap out of it, like waking from the haze of anesthesia, but I never did. I took no shots. I assumed no responsibility. I made no difference.

I vaguely remember doing all this on purpose so that if we lost no one could put it on me. Well we did lose, and no one put it on me, but who the hell cares? It was a stupid, meaningless, pickup basketball game with my friends. What was the big deal? Why was I so afraid? For me, not jumping into the spotlight during a high-pressure situation was like Winnie the Pooh giving up honey. It just didn't happen.

I was scared, and not the monster-in-the-closet type scared, but the falling-into-the-pits-of-hell scared. Before this basketball game, depression had been confined to college. I only experienced despair when thinking about what I'd study or if I'd succeed at life whatever that meant. Otherwise it was a fleeting thought I forgot about. But not during this pickup game. In this game, it broke out of containment and infected other parts of my mind. Whatever "this thing" was, because at the time I had no clue it was depression, it grew in strength. It was changing me. It was breaking me, and I wondered if I was already broken.

You couldn't see any of this from the outside. If you looked, all you'd see is a guy that normally took three-pointers not shoot a three-pointer. A guy that usually passed his classes get his ass handed to him in the kind of way most would refer to as a "learning experience" because it was. You'd see a guy that looked good and happy and even felt that way most of the time despite the creeping depression.

But I was changing. I could feel it like a chill breeze on a summer day announcing the inevitable autumn. A clock ticked over my head, a countdown marking the progression of these depressive changes. Second by second, minute by minute, day by day they'd take over more and more and more of me until there was nothing left. I couldn't stop it. No one could stop it. The only way to beat this demon was to push forward proving I was worthy of my life before the countdown expired.

Junior Year:

Slipping Away

When I started watching AMC's hit show *Breaking Bad*, I didn't like it much. Not because the show wasn't good – it was awesome – but because I had a hard time watching Walt transform from a decent man into a murdering drug lord. He was the type of guy you'd expect to age into a cranky yet generally affable grandpa, happy to spend time with his family grilling in the backyard next to their pool. Then he got lung cancer. Desperate to leave money for his family, he uses his genius in chemistry to cook crystal meth with an old student of his. Walter's plan was to get in the business, make some money ($737,000 to be exact) and get out. But money changes people. So does power, and for the first time in his life, Walt had both.

Little by little, the man known as Walter slipped away replaced by his drug-world, alter-ego Heisenberg. He's obsessed with the money, with "the business" and the power it grants him. By the end of the show he's no longer a soft-spoken wimp, but a full-blown bad ass who'd plant a bomb in a nursing home if it benefitted him… The contrast between who he was and who he became is striking, yet it occurs at a nearly imperceptible rate. The evolution of Walter's character from a gentle grandpa to a cold-blooded kingpin feels inevitable, if not natural. He was always Heisenberg pretending to be Walter.

Depression felt a lot like that; like an inevitable and natural evolution into the person I was always supposed to be. Sure, there were plenty of "growing pains" in the beginning like there always are when we change. That's followed by a phase of confusion where we don't know who we are; we're not the person we used to be, but we're not yet the person we're going to be either. After that, evolution into full-on Heisenberg is inevitable.

I was in that confused phase heading into junior year terrified of what my Heisenberg would look like. I felt trapped, and I didn't know how to break out. Then I had an epiphany; I remembered I had a choice. I wasn't *doomed* to transform into Heisenberg. Screw evolution! Screw the inevitable! No such thing. I have a say in who I am, and in who I'll be. All I had to do was decide who I wanted to be, then choose to be that person.

The "Time I Woke Up in a Closet" Story

"Dude, you pumped?" my roommate, Luke asked.

"To turn twenty-one? Hell yeah I'm pumped," I answered.

"We can't drink that much," Joe chimed in. "I've got a lot of stuff to do this week."

"I don't want to hear that crap," I replied. "I've got an exam Tuesday, but you only turn twenty-one once. We're drinking."

"You don't want to study…"

"Why would I want to study?" I asked pausing for a moment to let Joe squirm in the awkwardness of his innocent question. "Because I got a 'D' in Mass Balances last semester and fucked myself?"

"Pretty much," Joe answered as the tips of his ears turned a shade of red, a sure sign he was embarrassed.

"Nah, I'm over that. Besides this exam is just biochemistry. It's an elective so no big deal."

Yeah, I probably should've dropped Mass Balances after bombing three quizzes in a row, but I thought maybe I'd be able to dig myself out of that hole. Turns out when you try to dig yourself out of a hole, you might just dig a bigger hole! Who knew? And while I went to town with that shovel, the fall course filled up. So I had to wait till spring semester of my junior year to retake the introductory Chem E course. Peachy.

"Just don't do anything stupid like these guys," Luke said pointing at an article on his computer. "These guys blacked out and bought plane tickets to Alaska on their twenty-first."

"That's baller."

"We're not doing that."

"No shit, Joe."

"And this guy woke up in his closet!"

"Lucas might do that."

"What the hell are you talking about? I always make it to my bed, unlike *somebody*."

"Hey!" Luke shouted. "That couch is comfy!" The three of us laughed. Whenever Luke got drunk, he slept on the couch. We had no idea why. His bedroom was closer to the apartment entrance, but he'd walk right past it and sprawl out on the couch. I, on the other hand, always made it to my bed. No couch. No floor. No closet. I made it to my bed; it was a personal point of pride. I said if I woke up in a closet on my 21st it'd be one of the most embarrassing moments of my life. (Insert foot into mouth in 3, 2, 1...)

On the whole though, things were looking up junior year. I moved into Beaver Hill apartments, a complex in the middle of downtown State College, with Joe and three other friends from freshman year. Our place was huge for a college apartment. It had a bedroom and small bathroom on either end, with a spacious living area, and an island in the kitchen that was perfect for drinking games. I don't get excited about much, but I was stoked to live in an apartment with my friends.

And I felt like I finally got my head screwed on right. Over the summer, I put a lot of thought into switching majors even as I took three more courses towards engineering (physics 2, Ochem 2 – the class I dropped after scoring a 12 on the first exam – and an Ochem lab). But I decided against switching. I kept coming back to the sophomore year sign I received that led me to chemical engineering. I took a leap of faith on that sign. I wanted to see it through.

So, I failed a class, so what? It was humiliating, but not the end of the world. A good friend of mine from high school, Alex, tried cheering me up by telling me I was on my way to the top. He told me every great success story starts with an epic failure, and that I had just had mine – he said the only thing left was success. I wanted to punch him in the face.

I was so over the romanticization of failure. Every time I so much as stumbled, someone stood over my shoulder like a smarmy sixth-grade teacher saying, "Well, you know, J.K. Rowling got rejected from 11 publishers before Harry Potter became a success. And Walt Disney was fired from his news-paper for 'lacking imagination'. Can you believe that?" Oh. Ok, I didn't realize it was that simple. I did Step 1 – fail miserably – so do I just wait for success to fall out of the sky like a unicorn gliding down a rainbow with a pot of gold hanging from its horn or what? Realistically though, what was Alex supposed to say? Was he supposed to tell me my life was over because I failed one class? No, he did exactly what a friend should do and of-fered encouragement, so I settled on Chem E and stopped the back and forth. Once I quit all the hand wringing, I felt steadied, like calm waters after a storm.

The night Joe and I turned 21, Kevin, a friend from our high school cross country days, came over with a handle of Jager to celebrate. I hated Jager, but I had a rule about alcohol whether it was top shelf or bottom barrel; drink it. I took a couple shots of the licorice-tasting liquid while we talked about the heydays of long-distance running. Between the three of us, I was the slowest distance runner. Joe and I usually started out together, but then he'd leave me in the dust halfway through the second mile, and Kevin had a habit of shouting, "Afterburners!" as he passed me in the third. I'll never forget the conversation I had with my coach as he tried to figure out why I fell off so badly after a strong start.

"What're you thinking about? What's going through your head in that second mile?" he asked me after one particularly poor performance.

"I don't know. How much more I have to run I guess."

"No, no, no. You can't think like that," he replied shaking his head. "It's a distance race. You'll burn out. You've got to break it up into manageable pieces. One hundred meters at a time. You run a hundred, you change gears. You run another hundred, you change gears again, and you keep doing that as many times as it takes until you're done."

That's what I began doing my junior year. I stopped worrying about the enormity of life and took it a hundred meters at a time. Why ruin my 21st birthday worrying about an exam? Why ruin it thinking about past failures? There was no benefit to that. There was no benefit to beating myself up over the past, or worrying about the future, so I stopped and enjoyed myself.

After rinsing down the Jager with a few beers, we headed to a bar appropriately named The Phyrst. It's the only bar in Happy Valley that lets you take shots on your 21st, which led people to believe it's the only bar that even allows you in on your 21st so everyone goes there. The hostess handed Joe and I the traditional green birthday hats, then took our picture for the birthday wall. Kevin and another friend, Orto, bought us drinks, and Joe and I were hammered in no time. We had a great night.

We sang songs with the band, played some pool, ordered drunk food, and headed back home early Monday morning (our 21st was a Sunday night. Not ideal, but hey, Sunday Funday). Our roommates woke up to us stomping through the apartment like a team of horses, but they didn't seem to mind; it was all in good fun. I laid down in bed, watching the ceiling spin as if it were a fan and thought about how great the year ahead of me was going to be. Then I was asleep.

A few hours later, I woke up to a nightmare scenario (fortunately I was still pretty buzzed, so I didn't freak out). I was in complete darkness, but the sun should've been out. My blinds were paper thin; even if they were closed it would've been bright in my room. Why was I in the dark? And why did I feel trapped in a box as if I were buried alive? I couldn't even see my hands! I tried reaching out to my right but hit a wall after extending my arm about six inches. I reached out to the left with the same result.

What the... Where am I? I reached above my head grabbing a handful of fabric.

What the hell... is this a–

My eyes flew open in shock. "No!" I groaned as I realized the fabric in my hand was a T-shirt. I woke up in a closet! Maybe if I was real quiet, I could sneak out before anyone saw me. I kicked open the door with my toe and wriggled my way free like a worm wriggling out of the ground in a rainstorm. Of course Luke sat at the kitchen table pouring over homework.

"Did you just wake up in the closet?" he asked barely hiding his laughter.

"Yeah... how'd I end up in there? I went to bed... in my bed. Did you guys put me in there?"

"Nah man. That was all you."

Talk about embarrassing. My roommates joked all the time about me falling asleep in the closet. Anytime I bragged about anything, like how easily I'd make a half-court shot, they'd bring up the closest. If I beat them in a game, they brought up the closet. If I hit them with a sick burn – closet. The closet, the closet, the closet. I thought it'd never end. Then one day, the jokes just stopped like we all forgot about it at the same time. It faded away and became just another funny memory.

The same thing happened with my failure in Mass Balances. Up until that class, I never failed at anything I actually put my heart into, at least not publicly. The shame was overwhelming, and I thought I'd never live it down, but it simply moved on. I picked myself up, dusted myself off, and prepared to tackle that class a second time. I learned from my failures, and therefore, wouldn't be doomed to repeat them.

I didn't know it yet, but I'd fall back on this memory when I was diagnosed with depression. Never in my life could I have imagined the sheer magnitude of humiliation I experienced when the doctor told me that the great Lucas Wolfe broke from years of untreated depression. That's not how he said it, but that's what I heard. I was the guy that *didn't* break. I could handle anything. Atlas struggled under the weight of the world, but I spun it on my finger like a basketball as if it were a joke. Until it crushed me. How do you come back from that? The same way you come back from anything – with time and effort. Eventually, the shame faded away. Embarrassment, even mortal embarrassment, passes.

The "Wishing I Was a Kid Forever" Story

When I was a kid, my family belonged to the local swim club. This club was unlike any swim club I've ever seen. It had two massive pools, a small waterpark with a bucket dumping station and a short tube ride, a basketball court, a shuffleboard court, a campground, a baseball field, and even a 9-hole mini golf course. It was an awesome place to spend the summer.

Most days began with Joe and I playing a couple rounds of mini golf with our cousins, Matt and Eric. We had the 9-hole course memorized, but we never got tired of playing. Every summer we strove to score a "2" on each hole; that was our Man-on-the-Moon mission.

The most difficult green on the course was hole number 5. On hole 5, you had to hit the ball up a steep incline immediately followed by a shorter, but much steeper, second incline. Over the second incline, the green opened into a medium-sized circle that gave the entire green the look of a backwards "P." The hole was located directly in the center of that "P," but that wasn't the flag-hole; it was just a tube that ate the ball and spit it out on another circular green a few feet below. The second hole was the flag-hole and was also located directly in the center of the green.

You had to think about how to play this hole. If you hit the golf ball too hard, it rode around the curve of the backwards "P" and shot back down to you like a boomerang. If you hit it too soft, the ball didn't make it up the incline. Even if you managed to hit the Goldilocks shot – not so soft that it didn't get up and not so hard that it came back down – it'd come to rest against the wall at the crown of the "P" leaving you with a shitty second shot.

The only real way to play that hole for a "2" was to bounce the ball off the wall on the way up the inclines so it zigzagged back and forth popping out towards the center of the backwards "P" at just the right moment. But this added a new dimension to the game. Now, instead of simply being concerned with how much power to put behind the ball, you had to worry about the angle too. Hit the ball at too steep an angle and it bounced off

40

the walls like a pinball machine and never made it up the hill. Hit it at too soft an angle, and it hugged the wall and came back down anyway.

I can't tell you how many times that hole burned me. I'd score a "2" on every hole except that one. So close! I used to be so pissed after missing that shot that if there were a giant clown head on the course, I would've smashed its nose off with my putter ("You're gonna die clown!" – please tell me you've seen *Happy Gilmore*). But, after a minute or two, I'd let the anger go and play again. I'd adjust, using my "failure" to improve on the next attempt. That's what we do with failures, isn't it? We study them. Learn from them. Use them to succeed on the next go around. That's what I planned on doing with my failure in Chem E. I learned from it, and now I'd do better.

I remember discussing this with my Dad over Christmas break. "So, you looking forward to this upcoming semester?" he asked as I sat in the kitchen sipping a cup of hot chocolate.

"Yeah. I am," I answered.

"And how do you feel about taking Mass Balances again?"

"Good. I feel good."

"That's good. I don't want you getting too bent out of shape about it."

"I won't."

"Remember, my grades were terrible. You've already done better than I ever did. You can do this."

"I know. I will."

My Dad nodded, then left me in the kitchen to finish my Swiss Miss. I didn't lie when I told him I knew I could pass the class. I saw it happening – imagined it, dreamt of it. The old-me, the version of myself I liked, that guy was back. He woke up sometime in the fall semester and reclaimed my mojo. I think it's because I admitted my failure wasn't a product of stupidity, but a lack of decent study skills. As I mentioned before, my memory is good, so my go-to study method was to memorize everything. That may work for biology and history, but not for solving complex problems in which understanding theoretical principles proved paramount. For example, it wasn't enough to remember the Ideal Gas Law if I didn't understand the circumstances for when it was applicable. I needed to learn the principles, not memorize step-for-step how to solve past problems. Failure taught me that lesson in the same way failing to score a "2" on hole 5 taught me how to better approach that green. And when I got better at the hardest green, I got better at all the greens.

As I warmed my hands against the hot mug, I looked around the kitchen at all the Christmas decorations. Annalees of Santa sat along the cabinets as if creating a scene from a Claymation movie; Santa hammering away at a toy train. Santa checking his nice list. Santa hoisting his bag of goodies over his shoulder. Isn't it amazing what we used to believe as kids? That a jolly man with a round belly lived at the North Pole and delivered presents all over the world while riding in a sled pulled by flying reindeer. How ridiculous! How wonderful! How wonderful to be innocent and free enough as to believe that. My life was so blessed, and in that moment, I was filled with gratitude for it. Yet despite my gratitude, an acute dread bubbled in the back of my mind like when you wake up in the middle of the night and know you're going to yak. You fight it. You bargain with yourself. You go to the bathroom "to get a glass of water." But you know what's going to happen, and you know nothing you do will stop it. Eventually, in a terrifying rush of heat and sweat, you'll fling the toilet lid up and puke your brains out.

That feeling in the back of my mind – it was a brewing panic attack. There was nothing I could do to stop it and I knew that, yet I fought anyway. I needed to turn back "on." I forced my mind to run through memories of my childhood like a sped-up slideshow, but I only saw bits and pieces of them before they vanished as if burned up.

I bargained with myself. I told myself I was tired. My mind wasn't turning off; it was getting ready for sleep. Yes, that was it! I just needed some rest.

I went to the bathroom "to get a glass of water" (not really, I'm just on this step of the analogy). I focused on the Annalees allowing them to fill my mind, then blocked out all other thoughts and closed my eyes to rest.

But my panic grew like a snowball barreling down a hill gaining in size and speed. There was no stopping it.

The ball of ice in my gut exploded sending shards throughout my entire body from the top of my head to the tips of my toes. A cold stone of despair weighed on my heart. My frozen hands still gripped the steaming mug of hot chocolate. Then I was falling. Falling off a cliff. Falling into a black abyss. Falling into Hell.

What is happening to me?!
You're ok.
I'm not ok.
You're ok!
I'm not ok!
Breathe.
I can't!
You can beat this Lucas!
I can... I can, you're right. I can beat this. I will.

Old-me, that tough son-of-a-bitch, wasn't giving in to this damned panic. He was like dry blacktop giving traction to an out-of-control car skidding on ice. He pushed pleasant memories into my mind to fight the panic – Joe and I finding a turtle stranded in the tall summer grass of our backyard. Riding my bike down the park hill. Fireworks over Magic Kingdom. Round after round of mini golf at the swim club.

43

On and on it went until I turned back "on" and the panic subsided. I was happy to have fought off the attack, but that didn't put much of a dent in my frustration. This wasn't supposed to happen anymore. Old-me was back; I was Lucas-Fucking-Wolfe again! Gone was the dithering pansy of sophomore year who was afraid to take a shot in a pickup basketball game; the panic was supposed to be gone along with him. Why did it still haunt me? How could this weakness still infect my mind when I felt so strong? What the hell was going on?!

If you told me then that it was depression, I would've laughed in your face. I still didn't have a clue that depression was more complicated than a childhood tragedy. I didn't know it was an indiscriminate illness that could affect anyone. I didn't know that in its moderate stage, depression comes and goes like the tide, making it even more difficult to recognize an already murky illness. As always, I tried to explain away my feelings. I told myself it was subconscious fear that I'd fail Mass Balances again. It didn't matter how confident I felt in my ability to pass the class, my brain knew I failed once and some part of it was terrified I'd fail again. And if that happened… goodbye life! Who wouldn't be a bit panicky about such high stakes? No big deal though; all I had to do was pass the first few quizzes and I'd be right as rain.

Even as I used this reasoning to calm myself, I knew it wasn't the whole truth. Something else was going on with me. Something I didn't want to confront. I wish I had confronted it. I wish I went to my Dad right then and told him something was wrong, but I didn't. Instead, I sipped my Swiss Miss thinking about how I drank it every day as a kid. I wished I could've stayed that way – that I could have been a kid forever because I never felt this kind of pain when I was younger. I didn't have the capacity to. There was a world beyond me, I knew that, but I couldn't comprehend it. I didn't know its horrors then. But now I did. Except my life was easy and there were no horrors so what was my friggin' problem?! I didn't understand why the world threatened to swallow me. I didn't understand that all of this was depression.

So, I wished I was a kid forever. I wished and wished and wished with all my strength as if that'd lift me away to Neverland. It wasn't a comforting thought, but it was better than facing the truth of why I wanted to be a kid; I wanted out. I wanted to be unaware. Just like that day at Beaver stadium, I was overcome with a desire not to die, but to end. To feel nothing. To *be* nothing. Why? Why did I want that? I didn't know. I didn't know how to confront my pain. I didn't know how to talk about it. All I knew was that it wasn't good to want out.

I wish I was a kid forever.

The "Fruitless Redemption" Story

"Holy–" James yelled as the sinking couch cushions he sat on nearly touched the floor. "What the hell happened to our couch?"

"Last night," Sumit answered. "Last night happened to our couch."

"Were people dancing on it?"

"I don't know that I'd call a bunch of football players jumping up and down dancing," Luke said.

"What? Why would they do that?"

"I dunno. What I *do* know is last night was lit!"

"Dude it really was," I added. "Can't believe we had some football players here."

"If Hackenberg goes pro, we can say we had an NFL quarterback at our apartment." I don't usually care about meeting celebrities – and the Penn State football players are celebrities in Happy Valley – but I have to admit it was cool having them at our party. And for the few minutes that I talked to Hackenberg, he seemed like a chill guy.

"That's coming out of our security deposit," Joe said waving towards the couch that looked like a broken-in-half ship.

"Can we worry about that later?" I asked, gently rubbing my temples.

"Hungover?"

"Yeah, like a limp dick."

"Ha, limp dick. Me too man," Sumit said.

"You want some breakfast."

"I could go for some food. And water."

"Here," Luke said sliding a glass of water across the island to me. I mumbled my thanks as I sipped the refreshing liquid hoping it'd alleviate the worst of my headache. At least I wasn't nauseous. Headaches I didn't mind; a little water and an Advil or two cleared those up. Nausea hung around all day like a bad cold.

The broken couch wasn't ideal, but it was the least of my worries at the moment. My condition throughout spring semester had steadily declined, which made no sense to me. For the first couple weeks after Christmas break, I studied like a workaholic on crack. Every homework problem, every class example, all my notes, the previous year's quiz. I went to office hours. I read the chapter in the class textbook two, then three, then four times until I knew the material inside out and backwards. I recited formulas in my sleep. I changed assumptions that guided example problems to see if I could still work out how to solve them under varying conditions. I did all of this because I needed redemption. That would cure me. That would cast out once and for all the panic that still plagued me. Redemption in Mass Balances was the gateway to my future, without it, I had no future.

Let's let that sink in for a minute – without redemption in Mass Balances I had no future. A bit heavy handed for a college class, don't you think? I thought so, but all the same, the class mattered that much to me. If I failed a second time, three years of college went down the drain with nothing to show for it. Failure meant all that I did to build a future was for nothing. Since most of my life centered around building a stable future, that meant my life was for nothing.

Of course that's not true. We all have infinite value outside of what we achieve, but I lost sight of this truth. Depression, for all its irrationality, possesses a cunning logic like the serpent in the Garden. The illness weaves absurd lies wrapped in a kernel of truth so we accept them. I knew people mattered outside of what they achieved because Gabriel mattered to me as much as anybody, and his so-called ability to achieve was near zero. In the abstract, I knew I mattered, but I didn't believe it. Only redemption could save me.

The night before the first quiz (which was three weeks into the semester), I barely slept. It wasn't because of nerves though; I buzzed with excitement like an athlete before the big game. I *wanted* to take this quiz. I wanted to grab it by the metaphorical throat and tell it that I had enough of it controlling me. I was taking my damn life back! And that's exactly what I did.

The quiz was easy. I didn't even ask anyone if it was easy; I knew it was, and I knew how to solve every question it asked. With roughly twenty minutes left in the period, I handed it in confident that I had slain the dragon. Now all I had to do was wait for the official grade to post a week later. Obviously that week crawled by at a snail's pace. Time always does when we need it to go quickly.

Eventually the days passed, and I shuffled through the pile of quizzes on my professor's desk along with everyone else looking for mine. The plan was to grab my quiz, head to a se-cluded section of the auditorium-style classroom, and sneak a peek at my grade in relative privacy. That didn't happen. Right next to my chicken-scratch signature at the top of the page was my grade – 100!

Fuck yeah! Yes! I friggin' did it! Mass Balances my ass. Stupid class.

That quiz marked my one and only 100% on a chemical engineering exam. I was over the moon about it! For a year, Chem E kicked me in the balls; now I kicked it right back in the balls. Sure, I still had six quizzes to go, but it's not always a bad thing to celebrate a few yards shy of the end zone (unless you're Desean Jackson!).

Even though I celebrated early, unlike Desean, I held onto the ball. I didn't ramp the intensity of my studying down one bit. I was so pumped by that first victory, so convinced that passing this class would right the ship and get my life back on track, that I easily kept chugging along without getting the least bit tired. I wasn't even discouraged when the nightmares re-turned. Screw em' was my philosophy. Any one of the remaining quizzes could sink me. Until I had a "C" on lock, the nightmares had a reason to exist. All I had to do was focus on redemption, and they'd leave me alone. So, I kept studying and studying and studying.

When the second quiz rolled around in early February, I was ready. Unfortunately, I bombed that quiz...

Nah, just kidding, I killed that quiz too! I think I got a 96 – something around there. And, I was doing well in my other clas-ses too, so it's not like I was bombing everything else to pass Mass Balances. In fact, everything in my life was going better! I began spring semester focused on redeeming myself academ-ically but wound up accomplishing much more. Erica and I were back together, though we still had to keep it a secret. We both tried dating other people in the fall semester, but it didn't work out. Despite all the problems we had because of circumstances out of our control, neither of us could forget the day Erica asked me if I believed in love at first sight. You just don't give up on a moment like that. So, we were together again, with no real plan for the future, but a shared determination to find a way for us to work.

Aside from classes, relationships, and partying, I was also active in THON which raised a record-breaking total of over $13 million my junior year. For those of you who don't know, and I didn't know until I went to Penn State, THON is a student run philanthropy that raises money to fight pediatric cancer. It's a year-long effort consisting of hundreds of fundraisers that culminates in a 46-hour, no sitting, no sleeping dance marathon in February.

There's lots of ways to get involved with THON, and I was on a Rules and Regulations committee which sounds really, really, boring, but actually turned out to be a lot of fun. It's a huge undertaking that requires massive, student-wide effort, but anyone you asked would tell you it was worth it. I even volunteered to be one of three security leaders on my committee, a job that consisted of extra meetings each week and more responsibility during THON weekend. The extra time commitment was incredibly difficult to manage with my jam-packed class schedule, but I wanted to be as involved with THON as I could because of my cousin, Courtney. She was diagnosed with leukemia when she was only 9 years old while I was a freshman at Penn State (I'm happy to say her treatment was successful, and she's been cancer free for a few years now). Her diagnosis was one of those life events that hits you in the face like a giant brick. It's the kind of thing you never expect to happen; when it did, I wanted to help so I joined THON to show her support.

Each year, when THON announced its total, Courtney thanked me for supporting her and all the other kids with cancer. You may find this hard to believe since I'm spilling my guts to you in this book, but I'm not a very emotional person. I don't cry much. I'm not a fan of feelings. And I'd rather stick a needle in my eye than watch a movie like *The Notebook*. That being said, I damn near choked up every time Courtney thanked me for the little part I played in contributing to THON's total. So spring semester kicked off with a record breaking THON, two A's in Mass Balances, and a renewed relationship with the girl I loved at first sight. Pretty solid.

Yet the nightmares continued.

Sure, there were five quizzes left if you included the final, plenty of time for me to jack things up, but I was frustrated. I was supposed to feel like my old self again. Why did the nightmares plague me? Why could I feel the panic building along the edges of my mind like a rabid dog scratching at the door to be let in? I couldn't get a grip. I felt my old self slipping away, and who I started to become scared me.

Screw this man. You're too in your own head.

I don't understand what's happening to me.

You just have to pass this class.

It feels like more than that.

What else could it be?

I don't know.

Because that's all it is.

What if this doesn't fix me?

It will.

But what—

It will.

I pushed the negative thoughts out of my head. No point worrying about what might happen – I had to focus on the 100-meter dash right in front of me. One foot in front of the other all the way through the finish line. I kept studying and working and grinding. When the third quiz rolled around, it paid off. I scored somewhere in the mid 80's, then repeated that performance on the fourth quiz. That gave me a good enough grade that I could've scored a 0 on the remaining quizzes and still pass the class! I was barely past the halfway point of the semester, and I accomplished my goal; I redeemed myself!

But the nightmares continued.

Now I was pissed. Why did this achievement not make a difference? Why did I continue to get worse? If Chem E and fear of failure were the source of all my problems, then why did a stellar performance in the class that haunted me not fix it? The answer is obvious now – because chemical engineering had nothing to do with my depression. I blamed my bad grades for why I felt so horrible because I had no other way to explain my pain. At least I could reason that bad grades caused stress because if I didn't do well, then I wouldn't graduate, and if I didn't graduate, I wouldn't get a job. Then my life would be totally screwed up (not really. It'd be a setback, but not the end. However, that reasoning appeared somewhat true, so I allowed myself to believe it). That line of thought went out the window when I passed Mass Balances and nothing got better, and that terrified me.

Again, a part of me knew something more was going on than just the typical hurdles faced in college. I wish I had the courage to admit that to myself, to believe that despite the great life I lived, my pain was real. But I didn't. How could I? There was no reason for me to be depressed. So I struggled with my grades a bit and worried if I'd pass my classes. So what? I keep talking about Chem E like it was this great weight on my shoulders, but really it was a gift. That's how I thought of it then, that's how I think of it now. I mean, I got to go to college, and

not just any college, but Penn State! I had the ability to understand extremely complex engineering problems that mixed
calculus, chemistry, and physics – that's not something everyone could do. I was blessed with talents and opportunities
beyond my wildest dreams, all of it handed to me on a silver
platter by accident of my birth, yet a soul-crushing sadness consumed me with such ferocity I wanted to end my life. Why?!
Where did this sadness come from? What the hell was wrong
with me?

This fruitless redemption marked the first time I proved to
myself that external achievements won't dispel the darkness of
depression. A common trait among people struggling with depression is their tendency to write off their accomplishments as
nothing. I think we do that because many of us set up these goals
in our minds as the "thing" that will fix us, and when it doesn't,
we're forced to believe the accomplishment of that goal meant
nothing. The alternative is to believe we're irreparably defective. What explanation would you rather accept? That your
accomplishment wasn't all that much of an accomplishment, or
that you're a fundamentally screwed-up person.

I went with my accomplishment wasn't a real accomplishment. It made sense. I mean, it was the second time I took Mass
Balances, I *should* be able to pass it. That course was still the
easiest Chem E course I'd ever take – if I couldn't pass it on the
first try, what were the odds I'd pass the rest of my much harder
classes on the first try? Pretty low. I didn't redeem anything. In
fact, I still had a long way to go to prove myself… Duh! I never
should've expected to feel better after passing just one class!
God, it was so obvious. The nightmares, the despair, the impending sense of doom – none of it would leave me until I
proved I could make it. Until I proved to myself that I deserved
to go to college, and that I deserved a good life.

My success wasn't fruitless, and I wasn't a broken person. All I had to do was move the goalposts to where they should've been all along; securing an internship and graduating. If I could get an internship, do well, and show myself I was ready for the working world, that would prove I could make it. And if I received the stamp of approval that is college graduation after a successful internship, I'd earn a good life. There'd be nothing left to be afraid of!

A quiet excitement electrified my bones with hope. I may have been slipping away, but I knew how to win myself back!

Senior Year:

The Breaking Point

By now, you've probably figured out that I watch a decent amount of TV. I've seen *The Walking Dead, Breaking Bad, Family Guy, Big Bang Theory, Dead to Me, Everybody Loves Raymond, Friends, Daredevil, House of Cards, Jessica Jones, Parks and Rec, The Punisher, How I Met Your Mother* (which had the worst finale of any show in history), *Lie to Me, 24, New Girl, Schitt's Creek,* and many more. Clearly, I like TV.

I've always loved watching TV, reading books, and going to the movies. I'm fascinated by how we become invested in characters and their lives. We can get so into a story we feel like we're a part of it. Why do we spend countless hours staring at a screen entranced by the lives of make-believe characters with fictional problems? Because we relate to them. We relate to their struggles, to their joys, to their heartaches, to the complexity of their lives. Some shows are so relatable, they teach us about ourselves. I think that's why out of everything I've ever watched *Lost* is my all-time favorite show.

I loved *Lost* because I related to its main character, Jack. Jack is a spinal surgeon who becomes the de facto leader of the survivors of Oceanic flight 815, which crashes on a mystical island somewhere over the Pacific. Despite the disastrous situation, he's able to calm the other survivors through his matter-of-fact poise and doctorly-bedside-mannerisms. He finds shelter, water, and food, and develops a plan to survive over the long haul while waiting for rescue. When danger arises from natives that inhabit the mysterious island, Jack doesn't hesitate to put himself in harm's way to protect the other survivors. He's a leader in every sense of the word except for one; leaders know who they are and what they stand for, but Jack doesn't have the slightest clue who he is.

Jack's tortured by his lack of purpose, by how lost he is. Frustration and anger simmer below the mask of the put-together doctor like magma in a ready-to-erupt volcano. The sheer intensity of Jack's emotion allows him to push himself much further than others, but sometimes that drive becomes a weapon of self-punishment rather than an exercise of will power. The show masterfully illustrates this complex aspect of Jack's character in the episode in which he meets his wife, Sarah.

The first time Jack meets Sarah, he's working in the ER and she's rushed in after a head-on collision. She was in terrible shape. Her back was broken, she had crushed vertebrae, and her spleen was ruptured. If she managed to survive, Jack told her she'd most likely be paralyzed from the waist down for the rest of her life. Sarah began to cry and told Jack that she wanted to dance at her wedding which was only a few months away. After seeing how emotional Sarah became at the thought of not dancing on her big day, Jack promised to fix her.

Soon after the surgery, Jack is seen running the Tour de Stad in a nearby sports stadium (the Tour de Stad is a training exercise where you run up and down all the stairs in every section of a stadium). Jack looked half dead, yet he continued to push the pace which caused him to trip and hurt his ankle. Another man running the same exercise, Desmond, stopped to take a look at it. The two got to talking and Desmond asked him, "So, what's your excuse?"

"Excuse?"

"For running like the devil's chasing ya."

"Just trying to work a few things out."

Ah, the classic non-answer answer. It's emblematic of Jack's character – and mine. His burdens are his to bear alone. He so steadfastly believes that, he won't even share what's eating at him with a stranger he'll never see again. But Desmond persists and gets Jack to admit he's worried about his patient, Sarah. Interested, Desmond asked, "What'd you do to her then?"

"Do to her?"

Desmond smiles as he scans the stadium with knowing eyes. "You must have done something worthy of this self-flagellation."

"I told her – I made a promise I couldn't keep. I told her I'd fix her and... couldn't. I failed."

We all experience frustration after failure, but this was about more than just failure. Jack promised to fix her, to save her, and he couldn't. He derives his self-worth from his ability to save people when others could not. Without that ability, he's nothing. And Jack can't let anything go. He holds onto every failure, every mistake. If anything bad happens to anyone on the island, Jack blames himself. He punishes himself again and again and again like he did when running the Tour de Stad. Despite all his courageousness, all his strength, all his stubborn goodness, Jack's pain consumes him. He doesn't know his purpose, and it breaks him. He falls back into alcoholism, abuses pills, and contemplates killing himself.

I got that, all of it. I was angry, frustrated, lost. From the outside, I looked put together, but I was restless and confused. I used these emotions to push myself the same as Jack did, but

I found no peace. I didn't understand where this inner turmoil came from; it was as if I woke from a dream I couldn't remember, but still felt all the emotions from that dream. The only way I knew how to handle it was to keep pushing forward, but everybody has limits. Jack broke and ended up on the edge of a bridge wanting to throw himself off. I didn't know exactly when, but I knew I was going to break soon, and I was terrified that I'd end up on the edge of a bridge too.

The "You Don't Get Two Mulligans" Story

"Mulligan!" I shouted as Joe, Matt, and Eric nearly pissed themselves laughing. We were playing chip and putt, and I completely shanked my shot on the 4th hole. The pin isn't even thirty yards from the tee and the green is about the size of a basketball court. If you can't get on the green on that hole, you really suck, and we screwed it up every time.

"No way, man. You already used yours. You don't get two mulligans!" Joe managed to say, even as he cried from laughing so hard. I threw my club in mock frustration. "Screw this hole! Every time!" Seriously, every time. We never got it on the green on the 4th hole because we sucked, and that's why we played with a mulligan. You've got to use it wisely though; if you use it early, there's always the chance that you hit a worse shot down the road, and then you're screwed because you only get one mulligan. No matter how bad some future shot is, you don't get another.

I thought about that mulligan rule a lot senior year as I struggled through my Chemical Reactors class. The pressure was on. This was another core curriculum course, so I needed at least a "C" for it to count. It was also a prerequisite to the senior capstone design class, which was only taught in the spring semester, and was required to earn your degree. If you didn't get at least a "C" in Chemical Reactors, it put you back an entire year! That already happened to me once because of Mass Balances; I couldn't allow it to happen a second time.

The thing was, I was running on fumes by the start of senior year and really needed a victory. After pushing the goalposts back in junior year, I had a renewed energy and hope that I could get better from whatever it was that ailed me. That hope led me to sign up for two Chem E summer courses, and to submit my resumé to every company that would take it. I wanted an internship. I wanted to graduate. I wanted my life back.

But the internship didn't work out; I got rejected from everywhere. I tried not to take it personally – just about everybody gets more rejections than offers – but at some point, it got pretty disheartening. I mean, when you're rejected from Dupont, Dow, Exxon, Shell, Sunoco, FMC, Green Mountain Coffee, Siemens, Air Liquide, Alcoa, National Fuel, Techmer PM, Albemarle, Ecolab, Solvay, Campbell Soup, Kimberly Clark, Proctor & Gamble, Johnson & Johnson, Schlumberger, Anheuser-Busch and many, many more, you start wondering if you're tenacious or stupid. Even freaking Maybelline rejected me. *Maybelline!* Most people studying chemical engineering don't dream of working at a makeup manufacturing plant, so I thought I'd be somewhat safe applying there. Wrong! I didn't even get an interview to any of these companies. Just straight up rejection. If I got one more email that read:

"Dear Lucas,

Thank you for your interest in our company. As you can imagine, we received a large number of applicants blah, blah, blah. You have not been selected at this time blah, blah. We encourage you to apply for future openings.

Regards,"

I was going to lose it. I think I genuinely would have preferred they just said:

"Dear Lucas,

You suck.

Regards,"

It would have been less insulting than the PC-loaded, diplomatic, lawyerly, non-rejection, rejection. There was too much beating around the bush. Just tell me I suck so I know not to waste my time applying to your company until my resumé isn't as pathetic as the final season of Game of Thrones. Meanwhile, as rejections flooded my inbox, Facebook blew up with people announcing they accepted a summer internship at one company or another.

"Soooooo happy to announce that I have accepted an internship at company so-and-so for the summer of 2014! I'll be working at their facility in (insert some place that sounds awesome, so anywhere other than Jersey). I want to thank everyone who has helped me get to this point in my journey! This summer is going to be so exciting, and I can't wait to see what the future holds!"

I was sincerely happy for everyone that got an offer, but that didn't help me any since I *still* couldn't see a future for myself. Everyone around me moved forward with their lives, and it looked like they did it with relative ease, while I sank in a pit of quicksand by myself. The more I tried to get out, the further I sank. Securing an internship was one of my two goals, one of the two pieces of the puzzle I'd use to put myself back together. When I didn't get an offer, the fire of hope that burned within me fizzled to a flickering spark. But I figured if I did well in my classes, taking one step closer to graduation, that'd be like throwing a little wood on the fire. I'd be able to hold out a little longer. That's why I needed to do well. That's why I needed this victory in my Chemical Reactors class.

Now let me just pause for a minute and make something crystal clear: **My depression had nothing to do with my failures in chemical engineering.** Nothing. I struggled with the illness before college, and I've dealt with it for years afterwards. It didn't matter what I studied. It didn't matter if I switched majors or if I didn't go to college or if I breezed through it. I was always going to battle this sickness because it wasn't a product of my circumstances. The battles I fought in Chem E were part of a proxy war I waged against depression, but I didn't know that until I went to the doctor and was diagnosed with the illness. Since I knew nothing about mental health, I grasped for a reason to explain my deteriorating condition throughout college. The only correlation I stumbled upon presented a loose connection between my poor academic performance and my years-long downhill slide. There was no other obvious cause since depression wasn't on my radar, but this correlation presented me with two, lose-lose options.

Option 1: reject the notion that my lousy academic performance bore responsibility for my descent into despair. That wasn't a good option. If bad grades represented the only external factor capable of explaining my condition, and I rejected that as the cause, the only conclusion I could draw was that there was something fundamentally and irreparably wrong with me. No one with a life as good as mine should experience existential terror to such a degree that it drove them to thoughts of suicide – unless there's something wrong with them.

Option 2: accept that my poor grades are responsible for my descent into despair. This wasn't a good option either as it had major, negative implications. The first implication suggested my character was so pitifully weak to be this distraught over grades, that it rendered me nearly irredeemable. The second implication suggested I was an unholy narcissist. Remember, I frequently berated myself for struggling with molehill-sized problems while people the world over, some of them in my immediate family, carried mountains regularly. Only a supreme narcissist could recognize the unjust suffering that surrounded him and not be moved to place his relatively minor problems in proper perspective.

The only upside to accepting Option 2 was that I had some level of control over my grades. Accepting Option 1 meant I was screwed forever. Nothing anyone could do would fix me since I was irreparably defective. But Option 2 allowed me to maintain a degree of power over my situation – at a price of course – and that price was self-loathing. How could I not hate myself? I had a perfect life and part of me wanted to end it because I got a few bad grades after a lifetime of straight A's? You'd hate yourself too. All the same, it was better than being irreparably defective, so I went with this option.

That brings us back to my Chemical Reactors class which I desperately needed to pass. I believed I could do it. By senior year, people understand what's expected of them. We know how long to study for an exam, how much time to put into homework, and when to go to office hours. We're not rookies anymore. The weeding out was done a long time ago; those of us left wanted to make it. We didn't expect anything to be handed to us, but I don't think it was unrealistic to expect a fair shake at this point either.

Dr. Mifsud, our professor, didn't see it that way. He struck me as an unmitigated asshole; the type of jerk-off that took pleasure in screwing people over like the guy who gives you a parking ticket three seconds after your meter expires even as they see you running to your car. What pissed me off right away about this guy was his refusal to give the class a syllabus. The syllabus was packed with info, the most important of which was the grading scale. I wanted to know what grade got me a "C", so if worst came to worst, I could aim for 0.1 above that. But Dr. Mifsud refused to give the class a syllabus, and as the first exam approached, I had a sinking feeling in the pit of my stomach that this guy was out to screw us.

So, I studied. I went balls to the wall because I needed to pass. In my mind, this exam was kind of like those checkpoints in racing arcade games. You're hurtling a thousand miles an hour all over the racetrack, but if you don't make it to the checkpoint on time, that's it. Game over. Your game's cut short and you never reach the finish line. Make it to the checkpoint though, and you get more time to reach the finish. And your car gets a boost. Win-win right there. That inspired me, and in a little over two weeks, I put in about 100 hours of studying. That's ridiculous, but I was hanging by a thread and desperately wanted to take some pressure off myself. I couldn't afford to tank this test because I couldn't drop this class. I already used my mulligan with Mass Balances. No matter how bad I did in another class, I didn't get a second mulligan.

When the exam was finally put in front of me after this studying blitzkrieg, my first thought was *Ah shit, I am so screwed.* Professor Mifsud, who I not-so-affectionately sometimes referred to as Professor Asshat, gave us fifty minutes to answer nine questions. Typical exams were four questions in an hour and fifteen minutes.

I'm screwed. I'm so screwed. What the hell!
Ok. Ok, chill. It's a test.

I'm gonna bomb! I'll never be able to answer all these questions!

That's part of the test. He knows that. He knows you can't fully answer all of them.

That's bullshit.

This is how the real-world works. Deal with it.

I can't fail this test. I can't. I'm barely hanging on.

Then don't fail. Do what you can. Do it quick, then move on to the next question.

Ok... ok.

I only managed to answer six of the nine questions, but from what my classmates said, that seemed to be the average. This was an exceptionally good sign; I was usually well below the average. Some kindling got thrown on my flickering spark of hope and the flame grew. I took one step closer to graduation, one step closer to putting myself back together.

Then, a few days later, I checked my grade on the school website. I scored a 34.

Wow! That sucks ass! God, I am the dumbest idiot – damn! A 34?! Really? Fuck.

I mean, come on! I put my heart and soul into doing well on this exam because some part of me knew it was a battle for my life and the best I could do was a 34. That's friggin' horrible. The only reason I didn't immediately implode was because I had the sense to check the average; it was a 37.

I was so overjoyed I wanted to put on a pair of goggles and pop champagne like I won the World Cup! Typically, I fell well below the class average, but on what was arguably the most difficult exam of my college career, I managed to stick the landing. That constituted a hell of a victory. Dr. Mifsud *had* to curve the class. There's no way he could fail nearly everyone in a senior-level, core-curriculum course that was a prereq to our capstone design class needed for graduation knowing that many students already accepted full-time job offers and would have to start paying off loans soon, right? Right?! (I'm sure you see where this is going).

We nervously piled into his class the day after grades were posted. An anxious quiet settled over the room as Dr. Mifsud began writing the grade distribution on the board. He blocked it with his body so none of us could see until he finished and stepped out of the way. Talk about twisting the knife. People's lives hung in the balance and this clown acted like he was revealing the contents of a suitcase on *Deal or No Deal*.

When he finally stepped out of the way, the class's reaction was immediate. Boos, and jeers, and a general cacophony of discontent filled the room. He set the grade for a "C" at a 65. A 65! And the average on his exam was a 37. That meant even the above average students were failing the class.

"Are you serious?" I said to no one in particular. "What a dick! Unbelievable."

"Wow. What a guy," Cody, a buddy of mine, said. "Dude, I don't think he's kidding. That's not right." The people around us chimed in with their two cents, all of them agreeing. Some students started crying. This is where older generations might say something like, "Millennials are pathetic. Crying because you got a bad grade on a test. Suck it up. When I was a kid..." Yeah, we've definitely grown up in an easier time, no question about it, but take a minute to think about what these students were actually experiencing. Many of us have heard our entire lives that if we don't go to college, we're essentially screwed. Without a degree, you won't get a good job, you won't have a good life. So, many people take out five and six figure loans when they're barely more than kids, work their asses off, study all hours of the night and day, play by the rules, do everything that's asked of them, and at the last minute when the end goal is in sight, some jackass with as much power as a mall cop rips the carpet out from under them destroying everything they've worked their whole lives to build. That's what it truly felt like. And when a student asked professor Mifsud if he believed his grading scale was fair and an accurate representation of the class, he replied, "Yes. I do think it's indicative of your laziness and incompetence." Good move professor Asshat. Throw some gasoline on that raging fire.

The backlash was extreme. Students demanded something be done. Even my parents, who drilled in me for 22 years that life is unfair and we've all just got to deal with that, were furious. The chemical engineering department seemed to agree a line had been crossed, and in an unprecedented move, they waived Dr. Mifsud's class as a prereq to the capstone design and opened a new class in the spring for anyone who dropped in the fall. That was great for most people, and I was happy for them when the department announced the changes, but it didn't matter for me; I was finished. I needed the boost of energy that passing this exam would've given me. When I didn't get it, I just couldn't fight the depression anymore.

There's a certain, minimum level of energy needed to keep depression at bay. It doesn't take much energy at first, but after a while, it feels impossible to summon the strength to deal with it. If you've ever seen a Rocky movie, think of it like one of his boxing matches. In the beginning of the match, Rocky's slugging it out with his opponent. They're throwing punches, hopping around the ring, moving and dodging. It's intense. But when they get to round 15, they're not moving and shaking anymore. They're barely even throwing punches. All their energy goes into standing, and they can barely do it. That's the minimum level of energy needed to keep depression at bay; easy at first, nearly impossible after a while. Well I was in the 15th round, and that failure in Chemical Reactors dealt me a knock-out punch.

In my heart, I knew I reached my breaking point. As I walked out of class and across Penn State's campus, I began to collapse like a dilapidated building. There were no more gears left for me to switch to, no more 100-meter dashes of life for me to run. Despair enveloped me like a furious, howling blizzard, and I sunk into Hell. All I wanted was to lay down and die so I could be free from it all.

I don't think I would have made it through the day, except that something happened to me as I walked back to my apartment that gave me the strength to hold on a little longer. This event was even more significant than what happened in my sophomore year which convinced me to enroll in chemical engineering in the first place. It drove the despair out of my heart, and for a moment, gave me peace.

I can't tell you what happened just yet. It wouldn't make much sense to you right now; there's more I have to tell you. Just know I took a leap of faith my sophomore year when I chose to study Chem E, and my failure in Chemical Reactors represented the final nail in the coffin for that faith. It was dead. It was no longer a leap of faith, but a blind jump made by a moron. Except right as that faith died, something happened to restore it. By the time I got back to my apartment, I was as sure as ever that I was on the right path. Despite the Hell I was in, the despair, the brokenness, I was on the right path. I couldn't see where it led. I couldn't even see one step in front of me, but I was still alive, so I took that step. And then I took another. And another.

The "Double-Black Diamond, Marathon, and Internship" Story

I'd like to tell you things got better after what happened to me on the way back to my apartment, but they didn't. My depression evolved into a much more powerful illness, kind of like when Pokémon evolve (haha what a nerdy simile, but hey, if the shoe fits). The psychological pain was so intense, it began to manifest itself through physical symptoms. For the first time since my initial battle with depression in high school, my day-to-day functioning became impaired, making the illness increasingly difficult to hide.

The first side-effect of breaking was that it hurt to think. I physically experienced pain when attempting to do schoolwork. And it's not like this happened after hours and hours of studying or because of sleep-deprivation or something like that. I'd read two words of a homework question and feel as if someone threw boiling sludge into my head. My thoughts came to me as if from a distance like they were shouted through a fog. My brain ran slowly, like a virus-ridden computer, and I'd struggle with simple tasks such as adding basic numbers.

The second side-effect I noticed was I could barely hold a thought in my head. I'm not talking about your everyday difficulty concentrating; this was some next level shit. It was like somebody reached into my head and snatched the thoughts right out of it. I'd be working on a homework problem when my thoughts disappeared like they fell through a trap door. I couldn't remember how I was trying to solve the problem. Couldn't even remember the question. Then I'd re-read the question and by the time I got to the end of it, I'd forget the beginning and have to read it again. And these weren't long, jumbled questions; they were two sentences. I couldn't remember two sentences! This condition is known as brain fog, and it's fairly common for those struggling with depression to experience it.

Not every day was like this. Somedays I woke up and felt great, like my old self. Other days I woke up broken. I'd flip back and forth between these two states of existence, but it wasn't an even split. If I was a betting man, and I am, I'd put my money on waking up broken. Even so, I was happy to have days where I felt like myself and vowed not to ruin the good times by wallowing in bitterness over the bad.

Fortunately for me, I woke up to a good day one early Saturday morning over Thanksgiving break. It was the day I was scheduled to run a marathon with Joe and our friends, Seamus and Alex. We all needed to have a positive attitude to get through the race because none of us had trained for it. That's right, we didn't train for a marathon. Most people prepare for over a year to run this kind of race, but we only signed up four months beforehand and college didn't afford us a lot of free time to go on long, meandering runs especially if you were failing half your classes like me. It didn't matter. I knew we'd finish; there wasn't a doubt in my mind about it. The only thing I worried about was whether or not we'd break four hours.

Most people didn't think we'd be able to finish though, and more than a few appeared personally offended by our "arrogance" in assuming we could. That pissed me off. Arrogance didn't drive me. It was faith in myself, confidence if you want to call it that. When I wasn't half-possessed by depression, when I was my true self, I believed I could do anything. I've been blessed to be surrounded by people in my life, especially my parents, who built me up and shaped me into the type of person who doesn't give up. Ever. Sometimes the more difficult and challenging an obstacle that lay before me, the more I wanted to tackle it.

Like the time Joe, Seamus, Alex and I went skiing in Vermont over Christmas break. Alex has a house up the mountains, so he's a seasoned skier, but Joe and me? Not so much. We'd only skied once before, and that was at Blue Mountain in PA which is really just a glorified sled hill. It's nothing compared to the towering slopes of Vermont, so we tried to avoid black diamonds and trails with moguls, but we got lost at the top of the mountain and Alex accidentally steered us to a double-black diamond with moguls.

We lingered at the edge of the slope like a bunch of nervous school children as a cold wind buffeted us. None of us wanted to be the first to cross the precipice of the double-black diamond. It's sheer drop, littered with moguls, was a recipe for an inexperienced skier to get seriously injured. We considered taking our skis off and walking down the side of the mountain, but that's not really my style. I didn't care that the slope was filled with strangers I'd never meet again; no one was going to see Lucas Wolfe crawl on his belly down the side of a mountain because he was afraid of getting hurt. So, I launched myself over the cliff, bobbing and weaving like how I saw people ski on TV.

Later in the day, when we were back at the house relaxing around the fire after dinner, Alex asked me what made me jump over the edge the way I did. I told him exactly what ran through my mind as I jumped, "Sometimes, when you're not feeling it, you gotta do a little of what you're not feeling, just to feel it." Joe and my friends laughed their asses off, obviously not expecting me to say something so dumb, but the quote stuck. A year later when we signed up for the marathon, Alex ordered T-shirts with that saying on the back. No one really feels like running a marathon, but once you get going, you might be surprised to find yourself enjoying it.

And I did enjoy it, we all did. We genuinely had a great time. The weather was perfect, sunny and in the low 50's, and people lined the streets for almost the entirety of the twenty-six miles. They carried hilarious signs, wore goofy costumes like the Teletubbies or Gumby, and cheered us on like they were our own family members. It was awesome to see all these people come together and express sincere excitement for one another. It'd be nice if we could be that way more often. I'll never forget it.

Joe and I finished the race in 3 hours and 48 minutes, handily beating our under-four-hour goal. We got a medal, a whole lot of high-fives from bystanders, and some pictures to put up on Facebook because – well, did it really even happen if it's not on Facebook? After that, we headed home and checked "run a marathon" off the to-do list.

The next few days involved a lot of laying around the house recovering from the run. My legs were shot, so I tried walking as little as possible. Whenever I needed to get around, I'd shuffle across the hardwood floor, and if I had to do stairs, I'd waddle like a penguin to avoid bending my knees or using my legs at all. On the third day of recovering, my phone rang showing a caller ID from Phoenix, Arizona. I thought it was a scam and ignored the call but was surprised when my phone buzzed a few seconds later indicating someone left a voicemail. Scams don't usually leave voicemails. Out of curiosity, I listened to it wondering if I'd be offered a free cruise to the Caribbean or an all-expense paid trip to Disney World. Neither.

I was offered an internship!

That made me happier than Ron Swanson eating a steak on a hunting trip. The company was Freeport McMoRan, a large mining company out west, and a few weeks earlier I applied to all 49 of their available intern positions (I really wanted a job). I called the number back immediately but didn't get an answer. *No! Are you kidding? You just called me! Oh shit! What if they offer the internship to someone else now? No, no, no, no, no, no, no!*

I forgot I'd have to leave a message as these thoughts ran through my head until the phone beeped prompting me to leave a voicemail. In a rare instance of me losing my cool, I left one of the most cringe-worthy voicemails ever:

"Uh, yeah hi. This is um… This is Lucas. You uh – um I just got a call about a, uh, an internship… with your company, Freeport, uh Freeport McMoRan." Even though I was by myself in the basement, my face flushed with embarrassment like I was in front of a stadium full of people. *Hang up, dude! Hang up! This is brutal!* "Please call me back to discuss the offer when you have the chance."

Discuss the offer? What does that even mean? At least you didn't say 'um' 500 times in that last sentence.

Thinking that phone call probably hurt me more than it helped, I flipped on the TV to put it out of my mind. Before I even found something to watch, my phone buzzed with the same caller ID from Phoenix.

"Hello?!" I answered.

"Hello, is this Lucas? This is Dianne from Freeport."

"Yes, this is Lucas," I replied my voice cracking from the nerves. I was still in shock that I actually got an offer, and I was nervous that it somehow wasn't real.

"Hi, Lucas. I'm sorry I missed your call," she said taking a pause as if thinking through how to best say what was coming next. *Oh no. She's going to tell me she just offered the job to someone else who answered their phone. Fuuuuuuuuuck, I was so close!*

"You said you wanted to discuss the offer. What exactly did you mean by that?" she asked sounding confused. I tried thinking of something to say that would make sense, like negotiating pay, but that was a ridiculous thing to ask as an intern, so I decided to just tell the truth.

"Honestly, I don't know. It's been a rocky road trying to get an internship, and I was so excited I forgot I'd have to say something after the beep."

Dianne got a kick out of that. She was cracking up and told me she completely understood. An internship is a big deal, I'm moving on to the next stage of my life – all that good stuff (side note: this experience really cemented for me the fact that just about everybody reacts well to humorous honesty that pokes fun at your own expense. I recommend trying it sometime if you're in a tight spot). Then she gave me the nitty gritty details. I'd be working out of Freeport's Tyrone site located in Silver City, New Mexico. I'd be making $25 an hour, which I incredulously repeated back to her to make sure I heard correctly (*25 dollars an hour!* I only made $7.50 at my last job. I was gonna be rich!). I was responsible for finding a place to live, but Freeport would set up a LinkedIn group so we could find another intern to room with – those kind of things.

After confirming the offer was official, a geyser of hope surged through me with such force I'm surprised I didn't blast off like a rocket right through the roof. I got an internship! One of the two goals I set for myself at the end of junior year was accomplished. I didn't expect it to happen, not at all, let alone as early as Thanksgiving. Maybe there was hope for me! I was broken, and I knew that, but this internship – it handed me one of the two major pieces I needed to put myself back together. It could save me!

I grabbed three Coronas out of the fridge and ran upstairs to find my Dad and Joe in the kitchen. They looked puzzled, no doubt wondering what put a spring in my step and why I randomly brought three beers up from the basement. Without saying a word, I popped off the caps and handed one to him and Joe. Then I raised my glass and said, "We're celebrating."

"Ok," my Dad replied with a smile. "What are we celebrating? That you ran the marathon a few days ago? Or is it something else?"

"We're celebrating... that I just got offered an internship!"

Joe and my Dad went nuts. They were ecstatic! They bombarded me with questions. Who was the job with? What was my job title? Was it a paid position? Where was it? I told them New Mexico and their jaws hit the floor. They didn't believe me until we took out my Dad's phone and dropped a pin in Silver City proving it was a real place.

The image that popped up on his screen looked like something out of a low-budget Western. A lone road snaked through a barren desert sparsely populated with stunted trees and prickly, withered bushes. The only "grass" we saw was brown and shriveled like it had the life sucked out of it in an instant. The picture was a far cry from the lush greenery we were used to in Pennsylvania, but an ugly looking terrain was nothing to complain about. I got an internship, and my life had a chance to be put back together. Who cares if it's 2,000 miles away from my family and friends and home? Who cares that I had no confidence in myself to perform this job? Who cares that out of forty-nine positions, Freeport denied me from forty-eight of them? If I could run a marathon without training, and ski down a double-black diamond covered in moguls without experience, then I could accept a job in New Mexico that I didn't believe I was qualified for.

But that didn't mean everything would just work out. Sure, I launched down that ski slope in a moment of pride and I nearly got killed. I zipped down the mountain like a lightning bolt, lost control, and missed crashing into a snowmaker by inches. Alex's parents told me that when they saw me careening down the mountain out of control, they actually planned how they would get my unconscious body down the rest of the slope to the hospital.

And during the marathon, around mile twenty-one, my body freaked out. I only ate half a bagel with cream cheese the morning of the race. Let me repeat that so you can fully appreciate how dumb I was; *I ate half a bagel* to fuel an entire marathon! I also refused to eat anything while running; no protein bars, no Gatorade gels, no other nasty crap that people eat when they run long-distance. Big freaking mistake. The sugar levels in my blood plummeted. I felt dizzy and weak, but the real problem was my emotions went way out of whack. I was so angry for no reason and spazzed on Seamus when he asked how I was doing. About two seconds after that, I almost cried. Tears welled up in my eyes, and I was about to bawl like a girl watching *This Is Us*. Only through my enormous sense of pride did I manage to stop myself. Apparently, low blood sugar can cause violent emotional swings and that definitely happened to me. At the next water station, I stopped being an idiot and guzzled down seven of those awful Gatorade gels for an instant sugar boost. I felt a lot better after that.

Skiing down that slope, running the marathon – I knew they were risks, but I took a leap of faith anyway. I had to do the same thing for the internship in New Mexico. I would have preferred a job closer to home so I could be around my family and friends, just as I would've preferred to ski down a slope without moguls. It would have been easy to say that chemical engineering didn't have enough in common with mining, that I didn't have the experience to take the job in the same way that I could've backed out of the marathon because I didn't have the training. But I didn't back out, even though I was terrified. If this job didn't go well, if I failed again, then my last line of defense against depression would collapse. And if it did go well, then maybe I'd earn the chance to pick up the pieces and put myself back together. So, I accepted the job and dared to hope for a better future knowing it may cost me my life.

The "Madison Holleran" Story

After the internship offer, I stumbled through the rest of fall semester like I was playing dizzy bat. The prospect of a job gave me just enough hope to cling to life, except it didn't feel like hope most days. It felt more like an obligation; a chore I forced myself to complete so if things didn't work out, I could justify my end with "I tried everything." Nothing like some chipper motivation to get me out of bed in the morning. Bleh.

Anyway, I trudged through to spring semester and got beat down worse than Average Joe's dodgeball team in the qualifying round against the Girl Scout troop. It was embarrassing. My plate was too full, my ability to function too low. The classes I took included the senior capstone design which was like working a full-time job, my senior lab, two 400-level Chem E courses, one of which was the Chemical Reactors class I dropped after scoring a 34 because I wasn't letting professor Asshat give me a "D," and racquetball. Racquetball was cool.

The first exam that semester was a comprehensive test covering all major concepts we learned in chemical engineering over the years. I got a 54.

Good work Lucas, you friggin' idiot.

Goddamn it. I suck ass at everything.

The second exam was the redo with Chemical Reactors. I studied just as hard for this exam as I had for any, but brain fog killed me. Some days I couldn't think as if sand was thrown in the gears operating my mind. On the days this didn't happen, I'd study for hours and hours only to discover the next time brain fog rolled in I hardly remembered any of the material. I took the test on an ok-kind-of-day, but I still bombed scoring a

43. The average was in the upper 60's. I'm not even going to write the tirade of curses I let fly that day because I think my poor Mom would faint.

The third exam was in my other 400-level Chem E course, which was about biopharmaceuticals and prescription drugs. I'll be honest, I wasn't smart enough for that class. I bombed; got a 48. Surprisingly, I wasn't mad about it. I could work with a 48 because I only needed a "D" in that class, and it was curved. Still, the second part of putting myself back together was graduation, and a 54 as my highest grade of the semester wasn't anything to write home about. My fire of hope was once again reduced to a smoldering ember. Like I said, I trudged along more out of obligation than conviction, but at least I continued moving forward. I still believed there was a chance for me to make it out of this alive.

Until I read about Madison Holleran.

One day as I scrolled through Facebook, an article caught my eye. It was about a shocking suicide committed by a young college student named Madison. She had the perfect life. She was a star athlete for her high school soccer and track teams (both sports that I played also) before continuing on to the University of Pennsylvania where Madison fulfilled one of her childhood dreams of running track at the collegiate level. She was beautiful, friendly, smart, and kind. Her family was large and loving. She had it all, just like me.

On January 17, 2014 Madison took her life. She was 19.

I didn't want to read the article; I didn't want to know what it had to say, but I couldn't look away like when you drive by a horrific car accident and can't stop staring. Whatever happened to Madison was happening to me, and as much as I wanted to run away from it, I needed to know.

Something in Madison changed when she went to college, and no one seemed to know what, including Madison. She only knew that whatever happened to her was irreversible. Her family became aware that she was unhappy, and while they were very concerned, they didn't think it was all that unordinary. The first year of college is hard for lots of people. It's a big change. You leave home, leave your friends, leave your family, your comfort zone. In a way, it's as if who you were gets erased and you've got to start all over again. Madison's older sister understood the difficulty of this transition because she was unhappy her first year of college also, but she transferred to another school, and things got better. The article recalls a conversation between Madison and her sister in which she says, "This is normal. People leave home, they're unhappy, they transfer – they figure it out."

Madison replied, "It's not normal. It's not normal to feel like this." The deep freeze of depressive despair overcame me, brain fog rolled in, and panic took over.

You've known this wasn't normal for years.

Stop it.

You know how this ends.

Shut up.

You can't be fixed.

I said shut up!

But I knew depressed-me was right, and Madison knew it too. She would've understood what was happening to me because it happened to her. Convinced she was the only person who ever lived who'd understand me, I longed to reach out and bridge the divide between this life and the next with such passion it pained me. I wanted to find Madison and tell her, "We don't have to die. You and me – we can figure this out. We're not alone anymore. It doesn't matter if no one believes us, we believe each other. Maybe, maybe together we can beat this." But Madison was gone, and my heart ached for the loss of someone I never knew.

Before she committed suicide, Madison saw a therapist and admitted to having suicidal thoughts, but the closest she ever came to a diagnosis was "battling anxiety." That meant I was totally screwed. When a professional can only label your condition with something as evasive as "battling anxiety" I think we all know what that means; nothing's really wrong. Whatever your problem is, it doesn't *really* exist. It's all just in your head. That's why I didn't want to talk to anyone about how I felt. That's why I tried to convince myself that my thoughts and feelings weren't normal, when in fact, they were just as normal as what everyone else experiences. I wanted an excuse! I needed an excuse so when I finally left this world I could do it believing it wasn't out of weakness, but that something broke in me and it wasn't my fault.

I didn't *want* to kill myself, but suicide had a certain allure after the breaking point in the way a bug zapper attracts a fly; you know it's bad for you, you know how it ends, but you're still attracted to it. I thought about killing myself all the time, but not of my own accord; the thoughts pushed themselves into my head like they came from somebody else. I'd be talking with friends when all of a sudden there'd be an image in my mind's eye of me hanging myself. When I walked through the kitchen, I'd see myself lying on the floor dying as blood poured out of a wound in my neck. When buses rushed by the street corner, I thought about how easy it'd be to step off the curb. I could pretend I was looking at my phone – the driver would never have time to stop. Then it'd just be over. The most horrifying aspect of these images was the look on my face as I died. I didn't look regretful as you might expect; I looked relieved. How the hell do you admit that?

These thoughts "proved" to me that I was irreparably broken, that nothing could be done to save me, and that my story would end with suicide. Our thoughts are a part of who we are, and as far as I knew, medicine couldn't fix that. I didn't understand how a chemical imbalance in my brain could drive the thoughts that produced my depressed half. I didn't know suicidal ideation was a common symptom of severe, untreated depression. I thought I was crazy, and I felt more alone in what I suffered than Tom Hanks in *Cast Away*.

As I looked around me, especially on social media, I "knew" no one else felt what I did. Madison must've known too. Other people though, with gushing Facebook statuses and exciting Instagram pics – they'd never understand why someone with a perfect life wanted to end it. Of course, if you looked at my social media accounts, you'd never know the pain I experienced either. You'd think I was as happy and put together as anyone because online we share the highlight reel. The good, the fun, the uplifting. We share our happiness, and who wouldn't want to share that? It's a good thing to share. The problem with social media isn't that we see the highlight reel, it's that we *only* see the highlight reel. We don't share our thoughts. We don't share our inner turmoil. We don't share the insecurities that cause us to squirm in shame. And that's fine, I don't think Twitter is the appropriate outlet to express the deep, personal issues we grapple with, but when you're depressed, you lose the ability to separate what's real from what's filtered, and that further traps you in the isolated prison of despair.

What worried me most about Madison's story though, is that she accomplished her goals and it didn't save her. She always dreamed of performing at the collegiate level, yet she committed suicide soon after achieving that goal. Why? Maybe that was her proxy war, and it didn't matter that she won because winning won't fix depression. Maybe Madison suffered from the same sense of worthlessness that I suffered from, because I think at the core of every high functioning depressive is a Mount Everest of guilt. I certainly felt guilty as hell. I did nothing to deserve the perfect life gifted to me; that guilt drove me to achieve in an attempt to fill the hole in my heart. I understood that I was equal in value to all others and was tortured by my inability to comprehend why I was given a life they were not. I wanted to right this wrong, but how? How can I deserve to live my blessed life? By achieving. By "earning" the royal flush of a hand I was dealt.

But I can't earn it. There is no accomplishment that I wouldn't give up in an instant to grant Gabriel the healthy life he was robbed of. There is no accomplishment I wouldn't walk away from to grant a better life to the millions and billions of people who are worse off than me. There's nothing I can do so one day I can say, "What I've done is so great, it justifies the life I was given at the expense of others so I may achieve it." I drowned in guilt, the same guilt that forbid me from simply throwing my hands up and railing against the world like a typical college stoner. I had to do *something* to earn my life, but nothing I did would ever be good enough. I was hopelessly trapped. There was no way out. In the end, I knew guilt would consume me; I'd leave the world believing I wasn't worthy of life and refusing to burden others with my pitiful existence.

Maybe that's what happened to Madison, and now it was happening to me. Her version of pushing the goalposts back was running on a college track team. When she reached that milestone, and nothing got better, guilt outweighed hope, and Madison broke. There was no room to push the goalposts further back, no other side with greener grass. Because at that point, Madison realized, as I began to realize, that nothing we achieved would make us worthy of our perfect lives. Her story ended in suicide, and so would mine.

But here I am talking with you, telling you I was wrong. I thought nothing could be done for me, that no medicine or doctor or treatment could save me, but I was wrong. I came back from all of it. From all that pain and hate and anger and guilt. And not to simply survive, but to live! I'm happy. I have hope, and joy, and love for this wonderful life that I almost lost. I'm at peace with what's happened, and after a lifetime of feeling worthless, I finally believe I deserve to live. I *choose* to believe that. You have to choose to believe that too.

The "First Letter I Wrote" Story

When I was a kid, I loved playing soccer. Absolutely loved it. The sport made me feel alive, especially when I played summer tournaments in blistering heat. My team called those conditions "Cyclone weather" (our name was the Cyclones) because we won most of our tournaments in the summer. That wasn't a testament to our skill, we were a fairly average team, but a testament to our heart. Whenever scorching temperatures caused other teams to stumble, we stepped up and played our hearts out. I took pride in our ability to perform in extreme conditions; when the going got tough, and others quit, we got tougher.

I'd like to think that mind-over-matter mentality is innate to my character, and maybe it is partially, but I think my Dad had a lot to do with it. He championed playing with heart above all else. He believed in giving your full effort in everything you did, or you don't do it at all. He used to tell Joe and I, "You leave it all on the field. Everything you've got. I don't care if you're losing a hundred to nothing. You give your all every minute of every game until the whistle blows. Leave it all on the field." That's what I aimed to do every time I put my jersey on.

When I was about twelve, we played a match against a team that was much, much better than us. We got blown out of the water. By the second half, the score was 10 to nothing, and everyone on the Cyclones gave up except for Joe and me. We played like we only needed a goal to win. We didn't care that the other team played keep-away; we fought like we still had a chance until the ref blew the whistle signifying the end of a humiliating loss.

I lined up at midfield as dejected as the Warriors after blowing their 3-to-1 lead to shake hands with the other team. As I moved down the line, I was surprised to hear their coach asking for players 21 and 30 (the number on the back of Joe's and my jerseys). I told him I was number 30, and I'll always remember his reaction.

He stopped walking, squared his shoulders to me, and bent down slightly to look me in the eyes. He gripped my hand as if I were the most important person on the planet, and emphatically said, "Great game. Great game." Then he did the same thing to Joe. This guy was a bit off his rocker in my opinion. I didn't know what the hell he was talking about – that game was horrible. I didn't score a goal or take a shot on net or do much of anything except run around like a chicken without a head.

I jogged back to our sideline and told my Dad what the coach had said. "Do you know why he told you that?" my Dad asked.

"No."

"Because you and Joe didn't give up. Everyone else did, but not you two even though you knew you were going to lose. You left it all on the field. I'm proud of you."

I thought about that moment as I watched joyous students, only minutes away from graduation, mill about on the floor of the Bryce Jordan Center. The idea of leaving it all on the field – that's pretty much the only reason I was still alive. The whistle hadn't blown yet but staging a comeback looked impossible. Even if the internship gave me a boost of strength and hope, I still had to graduate to truly cure myself, and that goal looked further and further out of reach. A few days before Joe's graduation, I failed Chemical Reactors for the second time (even if

I passed, I still had to go an extra semester because of how far back Mass Balances pushed me). I needed a 54 on the final to get a "C." I got a 52. So close, but close only counts in horseshoes and hand grenades.

I was happy for Joe though, and all the students on the floor of the BJC. They'd done it! All the late nights and early mornings, all the energy drinks and coffee binges, all the ups and downs, the sacrifices, the failures, the successes, the blood, sweat and tears; all of it leading to this climactic moment of graduation. You could feel the emotion in the room like a jolt of electricity. Gone was the stress of the preceding years and gone was the fear of an intangible future. Now, opportunity lay before them like an ocean stretching towards the horizon.

I saw Joe from the stands where I sat with my parents and the rest of the audience. He was next to our roommate, Luke, both of them moving to Arlington, Virginia in July to start their jobs at Capital One. Quite a few of their friends also accepted job offers from Capital One or happened to accept an offer with another company in the Arlington area, so there'd be a whole Penn State crew down there. I was happy about that. It meant a lot to me that Joe wouldn't be alone since I didn't believe I'd make it much longer.

It's odd being a twin. I didn't think about it when I was younger because being a twin felt normal to me. I didn't know what it was like to not be a twin; to not be on the same sports teams, to not be in the same grade, to not share every moment of my life with another person. I mean, Joe and I knew each other since before we were born for crying out loud! We were best friends. How could I just leave him?

He needed to know it wasn't his fault, and so did the rest of my family. As much as I avoided thinking about suicide letters like a former alcoholic avoids bars, the fact that I had to leave something behind weighed on my mind often. I wanted them to have an explanation, something that allowed them to find peace and move on when I didn't make it. So intense was this desire, that one night a few weeks before graduation, I admitted to Erica I knew something was wrong with me. Of course, I didn't come right out and say it like that. She had to drag it out of me, and even then, I spoke in a deliberately vague manner so she wouldn't understand the pain I was in until after I was gone.

"Lucas," she said to me as I sat at the square table in her tiny apartment living room. "What's wrong? You can tell me." A small party at her place just ended, and Erica knew I wasn't myself because I hadn't talked the whole night. That never happened. I always talked. I never stopped talking. I talk so much that even Donkey from *Shrek* would probably tell me to shut the hell up. But I was too consumed with the war between depressed-me and real-me that night to talk to anyone.

"I don't know... I don't know what's wrong," I answered honestly. Erica took my hand in hers but didn't say anything waiting for me to speak again. We sat like that for a while as I tried to find the right words to convey what was so wrong with me.

"I'm scared. I'm so scared, all the time. But I don't even know what I'm afraid of."

"You don't have to be afraid, babe. Everything's gonna be ok."

"Maybe. Maybe not... I'm tired. I'm tired in my bones, but I have no right to be. I feel..." I trailed off once again searching for the right words. "Weary. I feel weary, like I've lived a long life."

"Babe–"

"I need to graduate," I continued in a shaky voice my eyes welling with tears. I told myself I wouldn't cry when I gave a piece of the truth to Erica, yet in the moment, my emotions threatened to overwhelm me. I took a deep breath to steady myself. "Something is happening to me. Every day I feel... I feel some part of me slipping away, and I don't know how to get it back. I just need to graduate, get away from it all."

Erica launched right into the encouraging girlfriend speech telling me I was the smartest person she knew, the best person she knew, and the most handsome person she knew (damn straight!). She told me she loved me, that I taught her what it meant to be loved, and that it frightened her to think about what she might have become if she never met me. All of that should've made me feel better, but none of it did. I was too broken.

Afraid that what I told Erica wouldn't be enough of an explanation for why I took my life, I thought about what I might leave Joe directly. He deserved at least that much from me. We both knew our lives would never be the same after college. We wouldn't live together anymore. We wouldn't see each other every day. We wouldn't talk or make jokes or work out or play video games or go out on weekends or do any of the dumb stuff you only do with your siblings because nobody would voluntarily be your friend if they saw how weird you really are. That part of our life was over. We both knew it, but Joe didn't know I planned on not sticking around.

Memories of our life together washed over me: warming our feet by the car heater in between soccer matches of one brutally cold Turkey Bowl tournament. Sitting on a bench by the side of the pool laughing like asthmatic hyenas at how we both nearly drowned trying to swim 300 meters for our lifeguard test. The summer before college when we stayed up late every night watching *Lost* or struggling to find all the hidden targets in Wii Sports archery. Our birthday earlier senior year when we wondered if we'd be able to spend it together the next year when I'd be in school and he'd be in Virginia. Not spending our birthday together would be a truly bizarre experience. Instead of a day of celebration, it'd be a day to remember half of us was missing.

That profound sense of loss and nostalgia inspired me to write a poem for Joe. An English class I took in pursuit of a minor focused on poetry, and my professor was all about us "interrogating our relationships" through the art of our poems whatever the hell that meant. Truthfully, I struggled in poetry classes because that type of writing is raw emotion, and I'm not an emotional guy. I don't like sharing how I feel but writing helps me organize my thoughts. When I write, the tangled mess of emotions swirling around my head condense into something coherent like a hot ball of gas condensing into a star. Joe and my family knew how awkward I felt about poetry, and that if I ever wrote a poem about them, it had to be important. So, I wrote one for Joe but never showed it to him or anyone until this book because in my heart I knew it was the first suicide letter I wrote.

Moving On
We run on the gravel path,
our breaths collecting in the frigid air
before we leave them behind
running through the woods our feet
pounding the trail in unison
step for step, breath for breath,
as it always is and always was for us.

Light on this late autumn day
fades into the shadows,
the fast approaching night.
We know that soon we will
have only the quiet babbling
of the river to guide us home.

I wonder how long we can last

knowing that we may never be
as we once were just as the river
flows in one direction
time will not allow
it in some other way.

Darkness falls and he runs ahead
I stumble on the unpaved path
my breaths unsteady, unmatched,
but he waits for me by the bank
of the river where we have
always ended our run

Again, bleh. I wrote this letter on a day when I was broken. I had almost no hope left that I'd put myself back together. Even if I pulled off the miracle of graduating after a successful internship, there was a good chance it wouldn't save me just as Madison fulfilling her dream didn't save her. But I couldn't give up yet. I had to leave it all on the field, and I still had more to give.

New Mexico:

How my Greatest Victory Tortured Me

"Lucas, there's something I want you to understand," my Dad said. We stood on the open, curved staircase of our newly built home. He was a few steps lower than me so we were eye-level, a sign he had something important to say. I was twelve at the time and dealt with a bit of bullying at school. Nothing terrible, but enough to hurt my feelings (though I'd never admit it). When you're young, you don't understand why people bully you, why they try to tear you down; my Dad wanted me to know why.

"There are two types of people in the world," he continued. "There are builders, and destroyers. The builders build things and the destroyers destroy what the builders built."

That didn't make a lot of sense to me. I understood why people built things. Building was cool. You made something, you created something. But why people roamed around destroying what others built – what was the point of that?

"Why do the destroyers do that?"

"Because they're jealous of what the builders built."

"If they're jealous, why don't they just build something themselves?"

"Because they don't want to do the work to be a builder."
My Dad paused for a moment, looking around our new home.
"Think of it like this house," he continued. "It takes work to
build this. A lot of work. You dig the ground away, lay the foundation, put up the frame, the electrical, the plumbing. It's hard
to build a home, yet builders do it anyway because they're willing to work to achieve something. But someone could walk in
here with a stick of dynamite, and in five seconds, destroy what
took years to build."

I believed my Dad – I remember believing him – but I
didn't understand why he was right. I couldn't understand why
people destroyed things; I was too young.

"You're a builder, Lucas. So is Joseph. People will always
try to tear down what you build. They will even try to tear you
down – turn you into a destroyer like them. Promise me – promise me that no matter what, you will always be a builder,
Lucas."

As I flew across the country to New Mexico, I remembered
the promise I made to my Dad; I'd be a builder, no matter what.
The time had come for me to rebuild myself; this internship
provided the foundation for a new-me. No more waking up broken. No more trudging through the day broken. No more being
broken. I may not have understood it was depression that
crushed me, but I knew I fought a battle for my life. So, I threw
down the gauntlet. I committed to leaving behind all those
thoughts of death, darkness, and despair. All those fantasies of
suicide. All that destruction. I was a builder! Time to build.

The "Sleep is for the Dead" Story

I woke up startled, the nightmare already slipping from my
memory like water running through my fingers. Fragmented

89

images of my dream danced through my mind; haul trucks tearing through the mine. Tons of rocks tumbling down the open pit like an avalanche. I was trapped somewhere. Then I was falling. It didn't make any sense, but I definitely fell in the nightmare because I hit the bed as if splattering on the ground and woke up. My heart galloped like a horse as I sat up, and my breaths were quick and shallow. The darkness of my tiny apartment in New Mexico came to life threatening to choke me.

Breathe.

You'll never–

Just block him out. Breathe. You're ok.

My lungs expanded like balloons as I filled them slow and steady. It worked. My heart relaxed, and I grew drowsy as the adrenaline wore off. I lay back down placing my face on the cool pillow and drawing the covers up to my chin.

See, you can fight it. You can beat it. You can win.

Well can we please win with some sleep? I'm friggin' tired.

I was exhausted. Even though I'd been on the job a few weeks, my body hadn't gotten used to waking up at 5 in the morning yet. It didn't help that I constantly had nightmares about getting killed on the job, though that wasn't surprising given how my first week of work went. That was training week at Freeport, and the only thing we seemed to learn about was how people got killed working at a mine.

Jorge, our training instructor, was a short, plump, Mexican man with a peppered mustache and the husky voice of an ex-smoker which appropriately added a somber note to everything he said. Jorge told us about people that had been run over by bulldozers. Run over by cranes. Crushed by dump trucks. Killed by explosions. Killed by flying debris from explosions. Electrocuted, and a hell-of-a-lot more. The most horrifying story he told us involved a haul truck accidentally running over a Ford

F-150 (the typical work truck driven around the mine) with the driver still in it. A haul truck is basically a house on wheels, big-ass wheels I might add. The thing's nearly 30ft tall, and it's capable of hauling hundreds of tons of rock. It's a monster. A haul truck could pancake a Ford as easily as you'd step on an ant, and that's exactly what happened.

"The driver quit his job the same day," Jorge told us. "Three years later he killed himself. Couldn't take the guilt."

What the hell kind of job is this?

"That's some messed up stuff," Justin, my roommate, said. I met Justin through Freeport's summer intern LinkedIn group. He had a car and agreed to drive me to and from work since I found a cheap, two-bedroom apartment for us. The deal worked perfectly because my car never would have made it across the country, and it was way too expensive to rent one all summer since I wasn't twenty-five. Besides, Justin was from Canada, so I figured he'd be a decent roommate because Canadians are generally nice.

Jorge continued with his sermon on safety, but I tried to tune him out after he mentioned suicide. I clammed up at the mention of it like a turtle hiding in its shell. I didn't want to think about death in New Mexico; I was supposed to leave that part of myself behind. This was my time to rebuild! But I couldn't tune him out. Jorge spoke about how that one, terrible accident affected so many people. Many needed counseling to deal with the emotional stress. Two people died; one the day of the accident, the other three years later by his own hand. The haul truck driver's suicide devastated his family and forced the community to relive the trauma of the initial accident.

That's what you're gonna do to them.

No I'm not.

You're gonna kill yourself. You know you will.

No. I won't.

It's the only way you get out of this.
Go away.
You have to–
I said go away!

I guess my depressed half didn't get the memo that I was done with him. He stuck to me like a shadow, sparring with me every moment of the day. I think he resented my full-throated attempt to get rid of him, which led him to become more dangerous like a wounded animal. The only reprieve I got from his constant siege was when I was with Sarah, the other intern who worked at the SX/EW section of the mine with me (SX/EW stands for solution extraction and electrowinning which is the process Freeport utilized to turn raw materials into a useable product). We worked in a set of dingy trailers that sat in the middle of the mine like a cold sore. Not many people worked there, and those who did had their own office, so most of my time was spent alone making it easy for depression to wage its assault against me until Sarah began work a few weeks after I did.

Our bosses, Jerry and Nancy, told me to show her around. The only job I performed those first few weeks was collection of the aqueous phase, a watery substance used in the copper-making process, so I showed Sarah how to do that. Large, open tanks that looked like boxes with their tops cut off churned the aqueous phase through a set of filters to remove gunk. Our job consisted of sticking a pole with a test tube on the end into the liquid after it passed through the filters. Then we took those test tubes to a closet-sized room with a centrifuge that spun the tubes at a high speed to separate the different materials within. That allowed us to measure the volume of gunk remaining in the aqueous phase after passing through the filters. Exciting stuff. It also took a while – about two hours from start to finish if you took your time. Sarah and I got to talking over those excursions and became fast friends.

The day after my falling nightmare, Sarah came by my trailer to see if I wanted to do the collections and found me nursing a cup of coffee.

"I thought you hated coffee."

"I do," I replied taking a sip. "Tastes like mud."

"And you're drinking it because?"

"Because I'm tired as shit."

"Yeah, you look like shit," Sarah said. I glanced at her to find her smiling. Just a joke, but I was glad for that because I felt like hell and was afraid I looked it too. Deep bags hung under my eyes like the droopy cheeks of a bloodhound. It wasn't exactly a professional look. It wasn't a young person's look either. Despite my best efforts to ward off depression during the day, I could do nothing about the horrific dreams I suffered at night. It wasn't unusual for me to wake up 4, 5, or 6 times. Each terrifying jolt to consciousness was accompanied by a battle to put down a mounting panic attack.

"So, did they give you a project yet?" Sarah asked when we began scooping the samples from the first of six tanks.

"Nope."

"Like what the fuck. Everyone else has one, even me and I started after you."

"I don't know," I replied, pulling back the pole and holding the test tube up. The liquid fell below the measuring line; I pulled it back too soon. "Gotta do this one more." Sarah held out her hand, and I gave her the pole to do the collections.

"Did you talk to Jerry about it?"

"Yeah."

"What'd he say?"

"Same as always, 'We're working on it.'" I looked around the mine as Sarah continued pulling in the test tubes. The surrounding landscape consisted of desolate piles of rocks, most of them covered in a foul-smelling solution used for leaching copper, the rest covered in a reddish dust kicked up by various trucks rumbling about the mine. Normally, the thought of not having a project was enough to induce a panic attack; I needed a project for the internship to go well, and I needed the internship to go well to rebuild my life. This was one of my two goals, one of the two battles I fought in the proxy war to earn my right to life. But when I was around Sarah, the panic didn't happen. I sensed it nearby, like an intruder at the door, but it couldn't get in, it couldn't consume me. My friends and family had this effect on me as well, that's why I tried desperately to always be around people and talking with them, but in New Mexico, only Sarah brought me this reprieve from Hell.

We changed the subject as we continued collecting our samples to talk about casino games and basic strategy for Blackjack. Sarah told me she never really played, so I taught her the rules and told her of some wild hands I'd been dealt over the years. When we finished recording the gunk levels, we went back to our respective trailers until the end of the day.

I spent most of that time in a paralyzing battle against my depressed half, trying not to let anxiety about the internship overwhelm me. It was difficult because I didn't feel like I had much hope to hold onto after failing Chemical Reactors by two points before heading out to New Mexico. Graduation looked out of reach, so if the internship didn't go well, then I had nothing. That would suck. I needed to change the equation, tilt circumstances in my favor. I decided to send my Chemical Reactors professor an email after work asking if we could review the final. I explained I only needed two points to pass the class, and that I'd like to make the case for those two points. This didn't sound like an unreasonable request to me since the class was made up of about a thousand points between exams and homework; two was less than half a percent of the total grade.

After sending that email, I checked my inbox about every five minutes for the rest of the evening. Surprise, surprise I didn't get a response because my professor probably had a life. That didn't help my anxiety though, which ran rampant like a rabid pack of mad dogs. Nothing to do but head to bed and hope for some sleep I told myself. Maybe I'd get a response within the week; that was the best I could ask for in the summer.

I fell asleep, but then I was at Penn State arguing with my professor for those two points back. He refused to give them to me. He stormed out of the room, and I went outside after him, but he was gone. I stood somewhere near Old Main but couldn't quite tell where I was on campus. As I tried to place myself, one of my front teeth fell out followed by a spurt of blood. I caught the tooth in my hand, looking at it in disbelief. Teeth weren't supposed to fall out at my age. Then another tooth fell out, and another, and another, and out of each empty gum poured a river of blood. It spilled down my chin dripping onto the sidewalk. I was bleeding to death. I tried jamming my teeth back into place. It didn't work. I shrieked for help. More teeth fell out. Panic engulfed me.

I woke up shaking, covered in a cold sweat (all my teeth were in my mouth though, so that was good). Another nightmare. Panic was no longer at the door; it got in and I'd have to throw it out before it took over. I pushed myself up out of bed and began pacing. I focused on my breathing, trying to calm my fraying nerves. I wiped my mind clean like a blank slate to block out thoughts from depressed-me, but it didn't work; he won. The fear of total annihilation swallowed me into an abyss of mortal terror. With clenched fists and gritted teeth, I sat on the end of the bed trying desperately to hold on.

God... please. I thought as my body trembled. *Help me. Please help me.*

Somewhere in the Bible there's a verse that says, "Ask, and you shall receive." Well I asked for help for a while, but now I begged. I couldn't go on like this. It wasn't humanly possible. Every minute of every day I fought depression, but now even in my sleep it tortured me. I had no rest. I had no peace. I was trapped.

There's only one way out.

Go away.

You always say, "Sleep is for the dead."

Shut up.

You want to sleep? You know the way out.

I did know, but I wasn't ready to take it. I had more to give, more to build. Maybe my professor would answer me tomorrow. Maybe I'd get my intern project tomorrow. I had to make it to tomorrow because tomorrow could be better. So, I sat on the edge of my bed the rest of the night, shaking, fighting, breaking, but still living.

God, God help me please.

The "Mrs. Cuckoo and The Copper-less Rocks" Story

"You can call me Mrs. Cuckoo," said the lady with the too-big-for-her-face glasses and a bob cut. She held a tall glass of water in one hand and stood with her head tilted slightly to the side mirroring the Shih Tzu sitting next to her. "All the kids do."

"Cuckoo?" I asked. "How'd you get a name like that?"

"Cocoa Puffs," she replied as if that explained it. Her dog nestled his head against her ankles like a cat. "I rescued him you know. Sometimes, I think he's the one who rescued me."

"Yeah, dogs'll do that for you." I'm not quite that sentimental, but I wasn't going to disagree with someone named

Mrs. Cuckoo. Besides, I liked her dog. He found me a few minutes earlier leaning against the stone retaining wall of their front yard as I tried to keep from passing out. I was on a run and learned the hard way what 6,000ft of elevation will do to you if you're not acclimated to the thin air. When her dog saw me struggling, he ran over and licked my hand a few times, then barked towards the house to get Mrs. Cuckoo's attention.

"You're not from around here. Working at the mine?"

"Yeah. I got an internship." I'm not from a small town where everybody knows everybody. I've lived in a large suburban area my entire life where you might know a couple people on your street and see a few familiar faces at the grocery store, but that's about it. Silver City wasn't like that. Everybody knew everybody, and everybody knew I wasn't from there.

"And you *wanted* to come here?"

"No. No, not really. It's two thousand miles from home."

"Ah. Home's back east then, yeah?"

"Yeah. Pennsylvania." I gazed out into the distance to where the mountain peaks threatened to poke a hole in the ocean-blue sky. "Don't see mountains like that back home."

"No, no you don't. I'm from West Virginia myself. Appalachia country." A silence fell between us as we both gazed at the towering structures of Earth reaching towards the heavens. Her Shih Tzu strolled over to me, and I scratched him behind his ears with my thumb and index finger. He closed his eyes and arched his head back and I swear he would've purred if dogs did that kind of thing.

"So what have they got you doing at the mine?"

What did they have me doing? Good question! Not my intern project I can tell you that. About a month into the job, Jerry banished me to another part of the mine (mostly to make it look like he gave me actual work to do) to help a couple geologists with a project they were in the middle of. These geologists, Garret and Lucian, were charged with determining if rock samples from a particular section of the mine had enough copper in them to justify processing the surrounding area. I was pumped! This project presented an opportunity for me to carry out real work. Freeport could've asked me to run chemical tests to determine the concentration of copper in the samples, a task which would look awesome on my resumé. Or they could've asked me to perform an economic analysis to discover under what conditions the project would turn a profit, another resumé-boosting endeavor. Is that what I ended up doing? Nope!

I picked up rocks. That's right, my job was to pick up a bag of rocks. Then, I weighed the bag, ripped it open, poured the contents into another, bigger bag of rocks, and threw that bigger bag into the bed of a truck to be shipped to Arizona for testing. I was furious!

First of all, I was pissed Jerry wouldn't give me a project already. I'd been at Freeport for over a month; what the hell was he waiting for? Secondly, I was not thrilled that he banished me to a far-away part of the mine where I wouldn't get to spend time with Sarah. She was the only person around who helped stand between me and a crushing black wall of Hell. What would I do without her? I wanted to stuff Jerry in a bag and ship him off to Arizona for being a shithead. But an apathetic boss wasn't something to get all bent out of shape over.

I had it pretty good, really good actually. Freeport paid me $25 an hour – an amazing wage. And this internship took place between college semesters; most people the world over didn't have the luxury of attending college nor did they have a decent job. They didn't live in a world of prosperity, opportunity, and freedom as I did. Most lived in destitution, hopelessness, and tyranny. I thought of the cartels running roughshod over the people of Mexico and Central America. The war-torn Middle

East and the awful killings we hear about and the ones we don't. The sex-slave trade in Africa and the genocides carried out regularly across that ravaged continent. Even where I live in America, most did not enjoy the same quality of life as me. They didn't go to top-notch schools their entire lives culminating in a paid-for college degree. They didn't come from a home built around family, love, and sacrifice. They didn't know the joy of believing they could accomplish anything. What the hell was I complaining about? That I had a bad boss? Boo-fucking-hoo. It's not like Jerry was a jerk-off ruining my life; he was simply apathetic. In the grand scheme of things, was that something to be pissed about? No.

So, I quit feeling sorry for myself and went to help Garret and Lucian with the rock-job. I promised myself I'd do the best damn job I could. No complaining. No whining. No bitching about basically lifting weights while wearing jeans and boots under the mid-summer sun in the desert (at least I wouldn't have to go to the gym after work). I even told my depressed half to shove it. That weasel whispered in my ear like a demon on my shoulder telling me there was no point to this job. There was no point to my life. There was no point to anybody's life. We were nothing but worker ants milling about somebody's farm scurrying from one task to the next all of it leading to… nothing. Those thoughts weren't conducive to a positive work attitude, so I told them to go screw themselves. There'd be copper in these rocks, and I'd play a small part in discovering that. That mattered. It had to.

The job got off to a good start. Lucian and Garret were decent guys, and we talked a lot because lifting rocks is only slightly more exciting than watching paint dry. We talked about college, working at Freeport, how we ended up there, where we were all from (Garret was from Utah and Lucian from Oregon). We talked about how the climate is different in different parts of the country, the absurd liquor laws in Utah and PA, and how crazy I thought it was that you could buy a rifle at Walmart in New Mexico. We even talked about politics, snapchat, and Pluto's demotion to a dwarf planet which they found hilarious because that really got me fired up (like who the hell woke up one day so riled up about the fact that Pluto doesn't "technically" follow the proper orbit of a planet that they actually spent their time lobbying for it to be demoted. And who the hell gets to make decisions about what's a planet and what isn't? I say we put it to a vote. Pluto would be reinstated in a landslide. The whole thing's horseshit. #JusticeForPluto).

Anyway, back to the rocks. The physical labor felt good, like exercising, but all day was a bit much. As the week wore on, depression took advantage of my exhaustion, delivering body blows and headshots while I simply tried to stay standing. Talking with Garret and Lucian warded off panic attacks, and I was happy about that, but they didn't have as calming an effect on me as Sarah did. And nothing stopped the nightmares. I thought maybe after lifting rocks all day I'd sleep like one, but no such luck. The equation hadn't changed. I still didn't have an intern project to work on, and despite multiple follow-up emails, I didn't have a response from my professor either.

Taking that into account, I think you'll understand why I laughed when Garret asked me if I wanted to pursue a master's degree after graduation.

"I'll take that as a no?"

"Yeah, that'd be a no," I answered placing a bag of rocks on the scale.

"It wasn't an easy decision for me," Garret explained, fumbling with the twisty-ties we used to seal large bags before tossing them on the truck. "I'll have to take time off work. Won't be getting paid. It'll be hard to go back to that."

"Amen," Lucian chimed in.

"So why go back?"

Garret shrugged. "I love rocks."

"Oh yeah? You wanna show these rocks a little love?" I asked as I pointed to the few bags I had left to load in the truck. Garret and Lucian laughed, then we all took a break from work to chug water like camels.

"So, what do you wanna do then?" Lucian asked me as we rested.

"Don't know."

"Well, what do you like to do?"

"Lots of things. It's hard to choose."

"You like picking up rocks?" he asked. I looked out over the dismal mine to the desert beyond.

"Can't say it was my first choice."

"What is your first choice?"

"Doesn't matter. This is all I got."

"Of course it matters, it–"

"No it doesn't," I shot back cutting him off. "This is the step I had to take to get to the next one. How I feel about it doesn't matter. Sometimes you just gotta do what you gotta do."

"You're right," Lucian answered. "Most of the time there's no way around that. But at some point, you've gotta do what you want to do, or you'll never be happy."

He was right, and I knew he was right, but there wasn't anything more for me to say. What I wanted wasn't any of his business. Maybe I didn't want to work at Freeport and didn't want to say that to people who worked there. Maybe I didn't want to get that personal.

"Yeah, well right now I want a shower cus I smell like shit." We all laughed, and the tension between us evaporated as we went about finishing up for the day. Lucian got me thinking though – what did I want to do?

I definitely don't want to pick up rocks for a living.

It's not that this job was beneath me; I was more than happy to do it in the short-term, but long-term? Picking up rocks? No, that wasn't enough. I could do more. I had to do more. There had to be something better on the other side of this Hell, something meaningful, something that made the pain worth living through.

There isn't.

Don't you ever get tired of being a pain in the ass?

The truth sucks sometimes dude.

That's not the truth.

Then why don't you tell me what the point to your life is? Why are you doing any of this?

I don't know. Yet.

That's what I thought.

What was the point of my life? Why was I doing any of this? Normal questions that everyone asks themselves from time to time, but depression warps these questions to become more than just curiosities; they become everything, the *only* thing. I needed an answer, but I couldn't give one. Without purpose, the utterly futile nature of existence threatened to crush me. Why did I choose to study chemical engineering? How did that choice give me the strength to bear the burden of life? Maybe by granting me the knowledge to accomplish some incredible feat like creating the next sustainable energy source? Or combining medicine and engineering to create new treatments for old diseases? Or streamlining manufacturing processes to reduce cost and energy? Would that earn me the right to live? Was I even capable of doing something so idealistic, of succeeding at a task of such magnitude? Or did I simply want a secure job that paid the bills and afforded me a little money leftover?

What are you going to do with a little extra money?

I don't know. Travel? People do that.

Travel?! That's the best you can come up with. You go through all of this so you can travel?

Alright, alright. I'd like a house. One with a yard and maybe a garden. And a fireplace.

That's pretty freaking selfish. People all over the world are dying of hunger – you can't even skip one friggin' meal – but go ahead, buy yourself a mansion.

Fine you prick. I'll donate it. Every extra cent I earn.

What'll that do? Help five people maybe. Then you can feel all good about yourself and pretend you did shit for people living through hell every minute of their miserable lives.

What the fuck do you suggest I do then?

How about cut the bullshit for two seconds and tell me what the point is?

I don't know! But it's not pointless.

Really? Even if you cured cancer, so what? Everyone still dies. All you did was prolong their suffering. You could discover the next energy source, solve world hunger, become the first trillionaire and give it all away – it won't matter. Not one bit. In the end, all anyone ever does after a completely meaningless existence is die.

I refuse to believe that. Life matters. Everything matters. There'll be copper in these rocks – that matters.

It doesn't matter. That's the truth. Sooner or later, you'll accept that.

My depressed half had me by the balls. I think he sat on that argument for a long time, waiting for when I was most broken to spring it on me like a boobytrap (see what I mean about the illness being cunning?). I didn't have a way to counter what appeared to be a logical argument. I felt like a flat-Earther desperately trying to hold onto my vain belief despite all evidence to the contrary. I had to. I needed hope. As I finished up the rock-job, I told myself over and over and over again that this job mattered, I mattered, everything mattered. There'd be copper in these rocks, enough for Freeport to mine the area. They'd be able to hire more workers and provide more opportunities for the employees they already had. There'd be copper in these rocks, and that mattered.

Mrs. Cuckoo's Shih Tzu trotted back to his place by her ankles, pawing gently at her knee to ask for attention. She chuckled as she bent slightly to pet him. "Like I said, he rescued me. I've had many bad days, tough days, but when I come home to my dog, it's ok because no matter what, we care about each other. That's all anybody needs."

"Yeah, I guess it is," I replied still looking off into the distance.

"Oh, I'm sorry," Mrs. Cuckoo said. "I interrupted you. You said you were picking up rocks?"

"Yeah, they wanted to see if there's enough copper in them to process another section of the mine."

"Is there?"

"No. No there's not." The test results came back earlier that week. The rocks contained trace amounts of copper, but not nearly enough to be profitable. My depressed half was right; the rock-job was pointless, and so was everything else. What did any of it matter? I thought this internship would give me purpose, that it'd be the first step in rebuilding myself, but it was just another step in a long list of steps leading nowhere. Graduation would be more of the same. It wouldn't fix me anymore than this job did. Nothing would fix me because I was unfixable. Maybe it was time to accept that truth.

The "Camping" Story

They say Hell is a bottomless pit, and I guess that's true, because every time I thought I reached the bottom, I found a way to fall further still. I thought I broke after my failure in Chemical Reactors, but that was really just a crack in the dam. I was able to hold out. But not finding any copper in the rocks – that lost me the proxy war, and now the dam burst. The village was going to flood. The only question left was how long before the maddening wall of water ravaged everything standing in its path. Fortunately, I was back at the SX/EW working with Sarah after the rock-job, so that slowed depression's ability to flood my mind. All the same, its physical manifestation worsened. On top of sleep deprivation from nightmares, I began to lose the ability to eat. Real fun stuff.

One weekend towards the end of June, I decided to join a dozen other interns on a camping trip. I figured it was better than sitting by myself in the apartment yelling at the router to work so I could watch Netflix. Maybe the outdoors would do me some good, you know? The healing power of nature and all that. Besides, I had never been camping, and when I was high on hope flying to New Mexico I vowed not to let fear control me anymore. That meant trying new stuff. Hiking with a bunch of people I knew for about a month to a campsite two hours from cell service? Sign me up. Shooting a gun for the first time during that same trip when I struggled to block graphic images depicting my suicide from appearing in my mind? Seemed about as smart as playing with fire in a room full of dynamite, but why the hell not?

We hiked the Turkey Creek trail and got lost somewhere along the way, never finding the hot springs that made it moderately famous throughout New Mexico. That was fine by me. After watching *Dante's Peak* and seeing a young couple get boiled like a couple of turkeys (pun intended) when they jump in a hot spring, I wasn't too eager to swim in one myself.

Eventually, we pitched our tents in a shaded area next to the shallow creek, then went about the business of setting up camp.

A few guys gathered firewood to cook dinner later, and a few more made quick work of a can of Pringles because we needed a target for shooting. Once everything was setup, we marched a short distance away from camp until we came upon a small ravine with a large, dirt backstop perfect for catching bullets. We placed the empty Salt and Vinegar can on a log against the backstop, then moved a few yards away in preparation to shoot.

I was nervous. I never fired a gun before, never even held one to be honest. I don't think I ever even saw a gun other than the one holstered on a police officer's belt. Most of the other interns were from middle America though, and they loved their guns. Just about everybody owned one, and they were all fluent in gun speak. Not me. To me, anything you can hold in your hand is a pistol and anything larger is a rifle. You try to get more specific than that, and I'm lost. I don't have anything against guns or people owning them, it's just not my style, but I said I'd try new things in New Mexico, and ever since my co-workers learned I'd never gone shooting, they were crazy about taking me.

Knowing they wanted me to shoot, I thought a lot about ducking out of the camping trip. Every time I imagined holding a gun panic gripped me, and I saw my life end in a splash of red. But I was sick of it. Sick of the despair. Sick of the fear. Sick of depression (which I still didn't even suspect I suffered from) ruling my life. So I didn't duck out. You've got to face your fears to get over them. At least that's what I reminded myself as the guys gave me a crash course in shooting – gently press the trigger so I don't jerk the gun, hold my arms steady with the sights lined up, exhale when firing for better accuracy. Above all, keep the barrel of the gun pointed away from yourself and others.

A couple of them shot before me to show me the ropes. I was surprised by the thunderous gunshot produced by a coffee-cup-sized pistol; the weapon looked like a toy, yet when fired, it produced a mature sound like an adult's voice coming out of a toddler. None of the shots hit their target. The Pringles can sat on the log, bored with our poor marksmanship. Despite everything, I found myself smiling, happy that I decided to go on this trip. Then it was my turn to shoot. The happiness didn't last long.

A colleague handed me the gun as nonchalantly as if he lent me a pencil. It was cool to the touch, refreshing even, like the river water against my fingertips. As he let go of the weapon, and it rested solely in my hand, the world around me dissolved into smoke. The guys shouted words of encouragement, but their voices drifted away beyond the reach of my ears. My palm faced up towards the sky, the barrel of the gun pointed down range. A quick flick of the wrist and it'd be pointing at me. Then it would be over. It would finally be over.

Not now. Not here.

The familiar panic sprouted in me like roots pushing through the soil. Usually it exploded through me, wild and reckless, but this panic crept with deliberate precision filling every nook and cranny of my mind and body. The sheer magnitude of despair threatened to annihilate me like a demon reaching up out of Hell to put a piece of it in my heart. My eyes grew wild. My breaths quickened. My heart raced. I *wanted* it; the freedom of death. More than anything. To know the bliss of ending this curse we call life. Despair turned to euphoria, dread to hope. I could rest! I could sleep! I could be at peace! All with the flick of a wrist, the pull of a trigger.

Do it.

Shut up.

Do it!

I said shut up!

DO IT!

NO!

BAM! The bullet ripped down the barrel of the gun slamming into the dirt backstop. I missed the Pringles can by about a foot, not bad for my first and only shot. Everybody slapped me on the back, offering congratulations while I handed the gun off trying to hide the weakness in my knees. I was dizzy and disoriented, the same as the day I wanted to jump from Beaver Stadium. But no one saw it. It was easy to hide.

Everyone else took turns shooting, then we headed back to camp to grab some drinks and take a dip in the creek running next to our tents. The weather was picture perfect; a warm sun paired with a refreshing breeze that kept the air from getting heavy and hot. We talked the way you'd expect a group of half-drunken guys to talk; ripping each other, lots of "fuck you's," and laughing so hard our sides hurt. I drifted in and out of the conversation like a bad radio signal not all that interested in talking and even less interested in drinking. The experience with the gun haunted me. I couldn't push it out of my mind, and it picked away at me like a group of vultures picking at a carcass. All I wanted was to run back to camp to take a second shot, this time aimed at myself.

I jumped up from the rock I sat on and placed my bottle of alcohol along the riverbed. I had to move. Death tried enveloping me like Mr. Smith taking over Neo in the Matrix; I couldn't just sit there and let it claim me. I had to outrun it.

The creek cut through a narrow valley surrounded by steep mountains on either side, so I decided to climb one. There was no path, no trail, no predetermined route. I simply ran up the rocky terrain using stunted trees and barreled bushes to propel myself onwards and upwards. Some rational part of me was afraid as I maniacally traversed the side of the mountain, but the rest of me just wanted to outrun the demons of depression, self-regard be damned! Maybe if I made it to the peak quickly enough, the beauty of the surrounding landscape would fill my mind before despair caught up. I didn't know what the view looked like from the top, but I believed it would be beautiful.

The physicality of the climb felt incredible like going for a light jog after a long, cramped car ride. My breathing became deep and steady, my heartbeat, strong as an ox. Endorphins surged through my veins. Sweat gleamed on my tanned skin like the sunrise shimmering on the surface of a lake. I pressed myself flat as a pancake against the ground as I climbed the last few steep meters to the top. Gravel embedded itself in my palms and sharp rocks scraped my knees; I didn't care. Even the pain felt good. I kept pushing, all the way to the peak, to the view that would save me from despair... But it didn't save me.

Nothing will save you.

Panic engulfed me once more, and my body shook despite the hot sun. This wasn't supposed to happen. This internship was supposed to help me rebuild. It was, without a doubt, my greatest victory. Grades could be marginally improved. I could squeak by in my classes, but rubber meets the road with a job. That's why I never believed I'd get one; I didn't think I was good enough. I didn't think I had it in me. When Freeport offered me an internship, I was ecstatic because I accomplished what I viewed as the more difficult of my two goals. Maybe I wasn't as worthless as I believed. Maybe I could come back from this. But my greatest victory didn't fix me, and when it didn't fix me, it tortured me by stealing what little hope I had left.

You know how this ends Lucas.

What happened to me?

Let's not play that game.

I tried. I tried to do what I thought was right. I didn't want to waste my life.

But you did waste your life. You failed. You're a worthless fraud and you know it.

Maybe... but I tried to be more. Doesn't that count for something?

Don't act noble. You had everything handed to you on a silver platter and it still wasn't enough. No, you needed validation. You needed purpose. You disgust me.

So what now?

You know what you've gotta do.

I – no, I can't do that. My family would be crushed.

Shut up. Just shut up. They won't miss you, Lucas. You're an embarrassment to them. You humiliate them. All you've ever done, all you'll ever do, is disappoint them.

But they still love me.

Because they have to! Don't you get that! You're nothing but a burden to them. If you loved them, you'd do them a favor and take yourself out.

Erica. Erica would be sad. She'd be heartbroken. She loves... I love her.

Heartbroken? You've destroyed her life. You think you did something good for her? That you fought for her? You fought for you. Your selfishness destroyed everything good in her life.

That's not true.

Oh yes it is. You're not a builder Lucas. You're a destroyer. You destroy everything you touch.

That's not–

It is true. Stop lying. Admit you want it. Just say it.

I don't know what you're talking about.

Liar! Say it!

I don't know what–

SAY IT!

I WANT TO DIE! I WANT TO FUCKING DIE! Please...
Please! Just let me go. I don't care – I'll do it myself. Please!
Please just let me die. Please... please... please...

The "Naked Truck and Laxative" Story

So, things weren't looking great for me during that camping trip to put it mildly. However, a little while afterwards, my professor finally emailed me back, gifting me the two points I needed to pass his class with a "C"! I was so happy I danced some sort of a jig right there in the living room pumping both fists in the air like I scored the winning touchdown of the Super Bowl. The happiness took me by surprise. I didn't think I'd ever be happy again; I thought that part of me died when I admitted I wanted to die. But the gift of two points acted like a defibrillator bringing those emotions back to life. Hope flickered within me once more, though it teetered on a knife's edge. Maybe I could graduate, get my life together, rebuild. Maybe it didn't matter that I wanted to die. I could come back from that too!

A few days after the best email I ever got, Jerry gave me my intern project. I could hardly believe my luck! It looked as if I caught a break, like in the moment that I was about to drown a lifeboat appeared out of thin air to save me. My project tasked me with formulating an equation to determine the rate at which leach pads plugged. Let me explain. Leaching refers to an industrial mining process used to pull desired compounds, like copper and other precious metals, from ore through a series of chemical reactions. To accomplish this, long hoses are stretched across the expanse of a leach pad. Think of it like a Hershey bar; the individual squares of chocolate are the leach pads filled with rocks, and the hoses are the horizontal indents that separate rows of chocolate. These hoses have tiny holes in them that are spaced about two feet apart across the length of the hose. The leaching agent, a light, sulfuric acid, runs through the hoses and leaks out of their tiny holes wetting the expanse of ore contained within the leach pad. This solution pulls copper and other materials out of the ore before being siphoned off to another part of the mine for separation.

Leaching works well but has a big problem – plugging. During the leaching process, all kinds of gunk makes its way into the hose's tiny holes plugging them. Once plugged, the extraction agent can't flow anymore. So, plugged holes means less effective leaching. Less effective leaching means less copper extracted, and less copper extracted means less money for Freeport. See the problem?

Normally, someone monitors the hoses and once they are deemed overly plugged, they're replaced with a new set. Freeport wanted me to develop a more efficient system. My job was to create an equation that predicted how long a set of hoses would last before becoming too plugged. That way, Freeport would know exactly when to switch out old hoses with a new set without having someone physically check them every couple of days. I won't bore you with the details of how I developed this equation, but it required me to spend a lot of time on the leach pads taking measurements.

Working on those things sucked because a dress code had to be followed when handling sulfuric acid. I wore thick, acid-resistant pants and a long-sleeve shirt that was as comfortable as sandpaper. I also wore gloves that reached my elbows, and knee-high rubber boots to prevent the solution from slipping in over the lip of a regular boot. Add in the hard hat and safety glasses at 6,000ft of elevation under the New Mexico sun in July and – well, you can imagine how much I enjoyed working out there for hours at a time.

At first, I was happy to work up on the leach pads though, but as the days wore on, that happiness drained away. In its place crept the cold isolation of despair. I have no idea why except to guess that the chemical imbalance driving depression overpowered the temporary release of dopamine I received over my recent good luck. The dopamine wore out its welcome after a few days and threw me back into depression. Yay.

The nightmares continued. Sleeping really was for the dead. Or the living. Not for me though. I had a Schrödinger's cat situation going on; I was dead and alive like a zombie, except you could argue a zombie fared better than me since they at least had an appetite. Mine all but disappeared, and I shed weight like a contestant on *The Biggest Loser*. Whatever was going on with me psychologically, it was so powerful that physically, I was messed up in all sorts of ways.

About two weeks into this project, I was on the leach pads in the late afternoon struggling not to throw up and pass out. My head throbbed, and I felt as if it'd crack like an egg. I never had a migraine before but given the ocean sloshing around my skull and the light piercing my eyes like shards of glass, I'm pretty sure I had one that day. Which was weird because I had no history of migraines, had no family history of migraines, and had no reason to have a migraine. But there it was, and it was intense enough that I actually considered returning to the air-conditioned office without finishing my daily measurements. Then I decided I'd rather pass out than return to the office with my tail tucked between my legs and the child's excuse of a "headache" for not finishing my job.

I crouched against a boulder for support as I finished taking measurements because I figured if I passed out from that position, the fall wouldn't hurt. As the summer sun beat down on me, sweat poured down my back like I was sprayed with a hose. It felt as if it collected in my pants, which poofed out because of the way I crouched against the boulder, but I decided that was impossible because a person couldn't physically sweat that much. About a minute later when I finished recording the measurements, I stood up and realized I was half right; a person couldn't sweat that much.

Ho-ly fuck. That wasn't sweat!

Unbeknownst to me, I shifted the position of the hose running over the boulder when I crouched against it so that it leaked the sulfuric acid solution down my back. That's what I felt collecting in my pants, not sweat. When I stood up, it poured over me, and everything from my balls to my pinky toes burned like a colony of fire ants ate away at me. It took me a second to figure out what happened, then I hightailed it for the truck.

Fuck me.

Get back to the truck!

Get to the choppa! (Arnold Schwarzenegger voice).

This Goddamn leach pad's like running through a friggin' ball pit.

Is there a wash station around here?

Shit. I don't know.

Ugh, I'm an IDIOT!

That's not me battling my depressed half; that's just me having a little fun at my own expense after I did one of the dumbest things I've ever done in my life. And no one does dumb quite like me, so that's saying a lot.

As I got to the truck, I threw my stuff in the back and hopped in the driver's seat. Then I hopped right back out. Sitting, pressing my skin against the acid-soaked pants, made the burning so much worse. There were no wash stations around, and the nearest bathroom was a fifteen-minute drive back to the office. My ass was on fire! I wouldn't make it fifteen seconds. This crap had to come off; I'd rather walk the mine naked than let the acid continue chomping away at me.

Naked. Hhmm, there's an idea.

I didn't consider the absurdity of my plan; I just jumped in the backseat of the truck and began tearing my clothes off. I had a tank on underneath the sandpaper shirt because I've watched *The Office* and had no desire for my nips to bleed like Andy Bernard's when he ran that 5k. The tank was covered in sweat, no acid. I could use that to wipe myself down, but that meant I had to get naked in the back of a work truck. Not ideal. If I got caught, it'd be humiliating, and I'd be fired on the spot. The leach pad I gathered data from was located in the center of the mine, so it was pretty heavily trafficked. There was a good chance I'd be seen if I wasn't quick as hell about getting this done.

Trying to take my clothes off in the back of the truck was like trying to get undressed in a clown car. There was no room, and I didn't want to touch anything and get acid on it. To get the boots off, I stepped on the heel of one with the toe of the other and pulled my knee to my chest, not an easy feat since I've got the flexibility of a two-by-four. Then I did the same for the other and threw them in the front seat along with my sandpaper shirt. The ocean in my skull churned like a hurricane approached, so I took a second to steady myself. Then I wriggled out of my wet pants and boxers tossing them in the front seat as well. Finally, I tried pulling my tank off but struggled because the sweat caused it to stick to me like crazy glue.

Mother-fucking-fucker! Get off you stupid piece of shit!

With a final, adrenaline-fueled yank the shirt came free, and I began scrubbing myself furiously. Everywhere I rubbed, the burning subsided. Success! And better yet, no one saw me. At least I didn't think so. I picked my head up to look out the window and was relieved to see no one, but as urgently as I needed to get dressed, I couldn't tear my gaze away. Smashed rock, nothing more than mounds of gray and orange rubble, stretched before me. Beyond that, rust-red hills, splashed with dots of green trees, rolled towards the horizon colliding with the velvet blue sky. It was a beautiful scene, like something out of a painting, but what the hell was I doing there? What the hell was I doing working an internship when I should've graduated already? As I stood naked in the truck, I began laughing. I laughed, and I laughed, and I laughed. The irony of the moment got to me. Joe started his job at Capital One a few weeks earlier, earning money and making life moves. A little bit before him, Erica began work at a fabulous company in New York City, a dream of hers since the day I met her. A friend from college, Gabe, got married a week after graduation, then headed to California with his newly wed wife to begin their life together. And where was I? Naked in the back of a truck rubbing my balls with a sweaty tank.

I tied the tank around my waist as a makeshift pair of boxers, then got dressed and headed back to the trailer-office. When I got there, I washed myself in the bathroom sink, then went commando in my clean jeans the rest of the day. Sarah must've seen me pull up in the truck because she came by a few minutes later asking how the data collection went.

"Interesting," I replied, not all that keen on giving away the details.

"How's the headache? I have more Advil if you need it."

"It kills, but I'll pass on the Advil. Thanks though. I think I just need to lay down."

"You wanna just chill in the office? I can go collect the samples myself. We don't need two people for that."

"Nah, it's ok. I'll come. I could use the distraction."

"Good," Sarah said with a smile. "It was boring without you. Jerry followed me everywhere. Fucking creep."

Sarah and I continued chatting through the afternoon swapping college stories and embarrassing moments from our teenage years. It was as pleasant an afternoon as anyone can have with a migraine, but I was happy when the day was over so I could go home. I plopped down on the couch and tried to shield my face from the light. I lay like that for a while until I thought about eating but didn't feel up to it and just went to bed. That night, I only woke up twice, and the relatively good sleep took the edge off the pain leaving me with a dull headache in the morning. But my stomach felt like a brick, which was odd since I hadn't eaten anything the night before. Maybe once I got some breakfast in me, I'd feel better.

I drug myself out of bed, poured a bowl of Frosted Mini-Wheats, and forced a few spoonfuls down. It hurt. I felt like I put a bowling ball in my stomach rather than a couple bites of cereal. What the heck was wrong with me? For a while, I sat at the table staring at the Mini-Wheats until they became so soggy, they broke apart like a sunken ship. Then I threw them down the sink and flipped the garbage disposal on. I knew what I had to do; I just didn't want to do it.

The last time my stomach felt like a ball of concrete, I ended up puking my brains out. I felt a lot better afterwards, but whatever virus I had then wasn't finished with me. The dreaded double-dragon visited me six times over the next few hours, and it was God-awful. Ever since that experience I was kind of a bitch about throwing up. I avoided it at all costs. But I didn't see another option here. I needed to eat. Before I could stop myself, I ran to the bathroom, knelt by the toilet, and stuck two fingers down the back of my throat.

Nothing happened. Well, I gagged a lot, but I didn't puke. I tried again. Same result. I grabbed my toothbrush off the sink counter and jammed it so far down my throat I hit the back of it and hurt myself. Still nothing. "What the fuck!" I yelled hurling the toothbrush at the wall. "C'mon! Throw up!" My knuckles turned white from gripping the toilet bowl. Each time I gagged a sharp pain echoed through my head like it was hit with a hammer. Snot ran out of my nose hanging off my face over the toilet water. "C'mon!" I stuck my fingers down my throat again. Nothing. "C'mon!" Again. Nothing. My body shook like I was feverish, my eyes watered from the force of the gags. "Please," I whispered as my eyes overflowed and tears streaked my cheeks. "Please let me throw up." Nothing.

I knelt at the toilet a blubbering mess for some time before cleaning my face with nearby tissues. Pushing myself into a sitting position, I leaned against the bathroom wall and took out my phone to Google the symptoms I experienced fully expecting WebMD to tell me I was dying (WebMD is so dramatic). Instead, it told me I was constipated.

No-freaking-way! I eat those stupid Mini Wheats every day. They've got like a hundred grams of fiber in them.

It didn't make sense. I drank tons of water, exercised regularly and was generally active at work. I ate fruits and veggies – stuff that's good for you and is supposed to prevent problems like constipation. And isn't that an old person's issue? I never heard of someone my age being constipated. Then I tried to remember the last time I took a shit.

Well it wasn't yesterday.

The day before?

No.

What about before that?

Nope.

What the heck! It's been like a week since I took a shit!

No wonder I was in pain! Curious as to what could've caused this problem, I scrolled down to the "Why This Happens" section and was shocked to see depression listed. And I knew, I just *knew*, that's what the issue was. All of it. Everything that happened the last few years. It was depression. It had to be! And while WebMD may not be the most reliable medical source, it's list of symptoms for depression was fairly main-stream. I had every single one.

Feeling sad, anxious or empty? Yeah. Feeling hopeless? Yeah. Feeling guilty and worthless? Uh, only for as long as I can remember. Not enjoying things you used to enjoy? Trouble with concentration and memory? Losing weight? Sleeping too little or too much? Thoughts of suicide? Yeah, all the above. That's me to a T. It made perfect sense, and no sense at all. Depression couldn't possibly be my problem. How could I be depressed? Nothing bad happened to me. Isn't that what causes depression? Isn't it from abuse, or death, or addiction, or some other horrific personal tragedy? Maybe genetics? But none of those causes applied to me, and just like the migraine, no family history either.

Confused, I put it out of my mind for a moment to deal with the constipation thing. That had to be fixed immediately. I got up, walked a mile and a half to the nearest drug store, bought a mild-strength box of laxative pills, popped one, and waited. The box said it'd take about four hours for the laxative to kick in, and expressly warned not to take a second pill if you didn't experience relief in exactly four hours (HA! Gotta love how they say "relief" as if we don't all know they really mean "shit your brains out"). Well, never one to shy away from an opportunity to do something dumb, I took a second pill after four hours and a couple minutes. A short bit after that I visited the bathroom and learned the hard way why you aren't supposed to take more than one of those pills at a time. I'll spare you the details, but let's just say it was so bad even the toilet cried.

That night I lay in bed feeling hollow like someone scooped out my insides with an ice cream scooper. I kept telling myself that I couldn't be depressed. I was Lucas Wolfe damn it! Lucas Wolfe didn't get depressed. I had too much pride for that. But really, I just didn't know depression could affect someone with a perfect life. So I lay there, wanting to die, and I told no one.

The "Biggest Mistake" Story

The remaining weeks of the summer dragged by largely without event. Most mornings started with a daily safety meeting, then I'd head out to the leach pads for a few hours. In the afternoons, Sarah and I collected samples of the aqueous phase together, then drove across the mine to park our work truck in its designated spot before heading home. I'd fix myself dinner, nibble on it like a mouse, then go for a walk while listening to Vance Joy or Mumford & Sons. When I got back, I'd go to the bathroom to wash my face, then stare in confusion at my reflection in the mirror. I didn't recognize myself. It wasn't me looking back, it was depressed-me, and I didn't know that guy.

Depressed-me had deep, black and blue bags under his eyes. His cheeks were slightly sunken, his skin had a hint of gray. Ribs poked out of his sides from weight loss. His eyes looked dead. They didn't shine with life or mischief, signs of the person I used to be. Those two orbs of sad despair betrayed me, because try as I might, I couldn't fake the life back into them, and people noticed something was wrong.

One day I sent my Mom a Snapchat, and she called me immediately and asked me to come home. She said, "Your eyes look so sad," but I told her I was tired, not sad. She was imagining things. I was fine, and she needed to stop being such a Mom because I wasn't a little kid anymore. I could tell by the tone of her voice that she was torn between trusting her instincts and believing her child. She must have shared those concerns with my Dad because a few days later he hinted I should think about coming home early too. That's out of character for him; he's Old Testament. He's the type of Dad that if I broke my leg, he'd tell me to walk it off which is honestly pretty funny. That's not to say he's uncaring, he just believed life was tough and sometimes to get through it you had to be tougher.

There's a lot I could tell you about my parents, and I feel like I've got to tell you something about them, because the stereotype for parents who send their kids to prep school is they're rich douches more interested in swingers parties than their children's lives. That's not my parents. They're the type of people who brought Gabriel home at 11-months-old when the doctors said he had no chance of living and loved him back to life. They took him to St. Katherine Drexel shrine for the nuns to pray over him, and soon Gabriel woke from his coma. After that, all bets were off, and the sky was the limit for their little boy struggling with impossible disabilities. And despite everything my parents had to contend with, they never neglected Joe or me. What I remember most from my childhood, is an overwhelming sense of family; a sense of family my parents built against unbearable odds. They never asked for a thank you. They never hung it over our heads or tied it around our necks. They're loving, attentive, compassionate, and strong, and they would've flown across the country at the drop of a hat if I told them I wanted to die. But I didn't tell them.

Anyway, I made it through those last few weeks by holding onto the hope that a good review at the end of the internship would boost my spirits. I didn't believe it'd fix me; that illusion died when I went camping. But when my Chemical Reactors professor gave me a "C," I felt good for a few days. Maybe a strong review would grant me a similar good feeling. And if it did, maybe I could ride that out to my final semester using it to do well in my classes. And if I did well, maybe each good grade would propel me up out of Hell with another boost. And if I earned enough boosts, maybe I could break free of my depression like a rocket breaking free of Earth's gravity. This was my last-ditch effort. My hope was no bigger than a drop in the ocean, but that was enough to hold on a little longer.

On the day of my review, Sarah and I picked our way across a leach pad in the morning to perform routine maintenance work. "How do you think it's gonna go?" she asked me of my impending assessment.

"I don't know. I'm a bit scared it won't go well."

"Why? You did a good job with your project even though Jerry gave you like no time."

"Are you nervous about your review?"

"A little."

"You did a good job with your project, didn't you?"

"Yeah."

"So why are you nervous?"

"I guess you never know what Jerry's gonna do."

When we finished our maintenance work, Sarah and I headed back to the SX/EW trailers for lunch. I had a few bites of a protein bar, then walked over to the office where my review was held. Chuck, Jerry's supervisor, sat behind the desk while Jerry sat off to the side against the wall. I was surprised to see Chuck, who hadn't been around for most of the summer, but said hello to him and Jerry and shook both their hands before taking my seat.

"How do you feel your internship went this summer?" Chuck asked.

"I think it went well. I learned a lot, and I'm grateful for the experience." I did think it went well, but the rest of my answer was a lie. I didn't learn crap. And I certainly wasn't grateful to have Jerry as a boss. He was as useless as Michael Scott without any of the man's redeeming qualities.

"Good. I'm glad you enjoyed it. As for your level of performance, we feel a bit differently." My heart plummeted into my stomach and there was a bitter taste in my mouth like wet ash. "Your level of self-sufficiency was much lower than we expected. It was rather poor."

Well that sent me from 0 to 100 in about a second flat. How could my performance be poor? It took Jerry weeks to assign me my project, yet I still completed it on time. I helped Sarah with her project. I did the rock-job. I did everything Jerry asked me to do and didn't complain once.

"How could my performance be poor? I finished my project despite getting it weeks late, and assisted others with their projects."

"You did very little on your own," Jerry said butting in. "If I didn't help you and give you many, *many*, clues you wouldn't have finished."

Do you ever have those moments where you and another person go through an experience and remember it *completely* different, except you know your version of the story is reality and whatever they're saying sounds like it came out of the Twilight Zone? That's what this was. Jerry did nothing for me all summer. Nothing. The guy didn't even show me around the mine properly which led me to drive onto a section that wasn't meant for trucks and I got stuck. There was no way I'd know I couldn't drive there since the entire mine was just a pile of freaking rocks – I didn't know some rocks were drivable and others weren't. It might not have been a big deal except for the house-sized bulldozer headed right for me. Fortunately, the driver was paying attention and didn't pancake me, but all safety incidents are reported in this line of work. A near-miss was filed, and supervisors and HR descended on the area like locusts. When they learned that Jerry sent a new intern out to drive around the mine by himself, against official and strictly enforced policy, he got harpooned by the higher-ups. The low review felt a little like retribution.

"What clues did you give me?"

"I'm not going to discuss that right now."

"Why not? I'd like Chuck to hear *exactly* what those clues were."

"Jerry and I have discussed your performance and have determined that your level of proficiency did not meet our standards."

"Yeah, you already said that," I snapped, struggling to control my rage. This was more than a review; this was my life and it was going up in flames before my eyes. "He doesn't even know how I did my project."

"Yes, I do."

"Then explain it."

"I'm not going to do that right now."

"Because you don't know.

"The review is final, Lucas," Chuck said ending the conversation. "We need you to sign this acknowledgement." He handed me my official review. I scored a two out of five.

A two?! What a load of horseshit!

Is it?

Yes!

That's exactly what a Millennial would say.

My depressed half had a point. Millennials are infamous for expressing righteous indignation over criticism they deserve. Maybe that's exactly what I was doing. Maybe I was the bratty, arrogant, incompetent Millennial older generations complain about. Wasn't it possible? My grades were abysmal. I barely understood any of the material in my classes. My only internship offer was with one of Freeport's most remote sites; no other sites, and no other companies extended an offer. All this evidence pointed to one undeniable fact – I sucked! I was a complete and utter failure. Why did I think I deserved a good review? I failed myself, my parents, Gabriel, everyone who didn't have the opportunities I had. I failed God and the life He gave me. My Dad was wrong about me; I wasn't a builder, and it was time to accept that. I picked up the pen and signed on the dotted line killing the last of my hope.

That was the biggest mistake I ever made in my life because hope is the most powerful force in the world. Hope can endure all hardships, all suffering, all pain. Throughout college, I always had hope. If I could just pass this class, or get that internship, or make it to graduation, everything would get better. I always held onto the hope that my pain was temporary – that it was simply the cost of admission to whatever reward lay on the other side. But then I went to New Mexico, achieving one of the two goals for rebuilding my life, and instead collapsed like a rotted tree. I hit rock bottom and lost hope. When I signed that review, I gave up on ever finding another way to rebuild. My hope was dead.

About a week later was my final day of work. "I can't believe you're leaving me here for a whole week by myself," Sarah said as I started the engine after clocking out for the last time.

"You got here three weeks after me. The way I see it, you still owe me two weeks."

"Yeah, but now we know how torturous this place is. How am I gonna make it without you?"

"One day at a time," I answered, steering the vehicle onto the dirt roads of the mine. We drove to our parking spot in silence. I used the time to think about how to say goodbye to Sarah. There's no debating it – I wouldn't have made it through the summer without her. How do you tell someone that without really telling them? How do you thank them for helping you stay alive?

"Well…" Sarah said when we hopped out of the truck in the parking lot. There was a hint of awkwardness in her voice;

I guess she didn't know how to say goodbye either. So, I gave her a hug.

"Thank you, Sarah. I wouldn't have made it without you."

With that, we went our separate ways, and the whistle blew. The game was finally over; I left everything on the field. Everything. A warm ember of pride glowed within me chasing away the icy chill of despair. I felt like a man who kept his composure even as he headed to the gallows, because I was only going home for one reason and it wasn't to be fixed. Graduation wouldn't fix me. This internship didn't fix me. Nothing could fix me. I was broken beyond repair.

I wasn't going home to get better; I was going home to die in a familiar place.

Choices:

Get Help or Die

Can you believe I didn't read Harry Potter until I was fifteen years old? I used to be a book junkie, easily reading upwards of forty books a year when I was a kid. But I didn't read Harry Potter until I went to high school and was assigned *The Deathly Hallows* for summer reading. I read all seven books in two weeks. You could say I enjoyed the series.

My favorite book was the 5th one – *Harry Potter and the Order of the Phoenix*. Harry struggles with his connection to Voldemort (the bad dude who killed Harry's parents and a lot of other people in the wizarding world). Harry's angrier than usual. He's frustrated. He has nightmares. Something in him is changing. These changes aren't good, and he feels powerless to stop them. His experience is eerily similar to depression; I was angry and frustrated and felt powerless to stop what was happening to me. Fortunately, Harry had the courage to reach out about the battle raging within him, unlike me.

"I just feel so angry all the time," Harry explains to his godfather, Sirius. Sirius was best friends with Harry's parents before Voldemort killed them. He's the only family Harry has, and he's a good man. "What if... something's gone wrong inside me?" Harry says in distress. "What if I'm becoming bad?"

That's what depression feels like; it's as if you're becoming bad and there's nothing you can do about it. The illness feels more like an evolution of your character than the onset of a sickness. That's why it causes such hopelessness – there's no magic cure for bad character. We can only change who we are by choice, but depression makes us believe we're robbed of that choice. Harry felt like he didn't have a choice either. Sirius knew better though. He knew Harry wasn't becoming bad, and he told him so.

"I want you to listen to me very carefully," Sirius replied taking a step closer to Harry and looking him in the eyes. "You're not. A bad. Person. You're a very good person, who bad things have happened to. Besides, the world isn't split up into good people and Death Eaters. We've all got both light and dark inside of us. What matters is the part we choose to act on. That's who we really are."

I forgot that. For so long, I felt powerless to fight the total assault on my spirit brought about by untreated depression. The illness may technically be a chemical imbalance in our brains, but it's also a siege of our will, tearing us down to the point of believing we don't have a choice; death is our only recourse from its destruction. But we always have a choice. Always.

I had a choice to make when I got home – the most important one of my life. Get help or die. Death would be the end, but if I chose help... if I chose help, maybe somehow, I could find a way to live.

The "Lightning Bug and Letters" Story

Do you remember catching lightning bugs when you were a kid? It was the greatest thing in the world! They only came out in the summer, every kid's favorite time of year (other than Christmas), and the simple beauty of nature entertained you and your family and friends for hours. I used to love going out in my backyard just before dark when the sun gave off the pale, orange light of dusk. The first few stars winked at you from the twilit sky and most animals of the day – birds, squirrels, rabbits, things like that – settled down for bed while the night animals would be waking up. Crickets chirped. Owls hooted. Bats flew in jagged zigzags, always one part spooky one part cool because you knew they were blind, yet somehow, they never seemed to crash into anything.

I remember a lot of those nights; running around barefoot in the backyard with my brothers and cousins. The fresh cut grass was damp and cool and comfortably stuck to our feet. The air had a sweetness to it, like honey and hay, and gave no hint of the fast-approaching fall. We'd carry empty jars of some sort, peanut butter or applesauce jars usually, and fill them with the lightning bugs we caught. Whoever caught the most "won" in one of those childhood games where there were no real rules and no way to win or lose. It was fun for the sake of fun and that was enough.

On one particular evening I only caught a single lightning bug. The first guy I snagged was absolutely determined to not be put in the jar. No matter how I tried to get him in there, he'd fly a few feet away, then come back and land on my hand a couple seconds later. I'd try to put him in the jar again, he'd fly away, then come back, and after a few times I gave up on putting him in the jar. If the little guy wanted to be friends so badly, then I'd be his friend.

I named him Lighty.

For whatever reason, I took Lighty on a tour of my backyard. I started by the porch where we had these giant forsythia bushes on either side of the house. "These are our big bushes," I said to Lighty. "They've got lots of leaves for you to eat." (I have no idea what lightning bugs eat, but I assumed it was leaves). I worked my way to the middle of the yard showing Lighty our swing-set, the dirty shed we never went in that scared me, and the tree with pointy leaves. "You don't want to get a ball stuck in here because the leaves can poke you and it hurts," I explained.

Then, I took him to the apple trees towards the end of the backyard. "Sometimes deer come here and eat the apples that fall on the ground. We don't eat the apples on the ground, but the deer like them." Lighty and me had a good time, and we walked around the yard for what felt like hours just enjoying a late summer night. Eventually, he flew away, and I told him goodbye as he went. After that, anytime a lightning bug hung around me for a while, I pretended he was Lighty and asked him how he was doing.

A few days after I returned from New Mexico, I stood in my backyard with Bolt, my family's chocolate lab, as he rummaged through the grass smelling everything in the way dogs do. The air had that familiar sweetness of honey and hay and just a hint of cow manure (I live near a farm). It was dark out; the faint glow of twilight slipped away unnoticed as the sun sank below the horizon. Lightning bugs lit up the yard like flashes from paparazzi cameras. I caught one as I sat next to Bolt who grew tired of sniffing and lay down.

"Hello," I said to the lightning bug. I didn't have the heart to call him Lighty; I felt too stupid at 20-something-years-old to do that. "It was a nice day today. A very nice day."

It was Gabriel's 21st birthday, and it really was a nice day. Gabriel loves birthdays, especially his, so we always try to make it a big celebration for him. He never gets tired of blowing out candles, opening presents, being showered with attention; the kid's a ham. And he deserves to be with all that he goes through; why not milk a little extra attention out of his special day?

"You think this is good?" I asked the lightning bug, showing it a picture of me and the family out for Gabriel's birthday dinner earlier in the evening. We went to one of his favorite restaurants and the waitresses, who absolutely adore Gabriel, brought him endless rounds of his favorite drink... chocolate milk topped with whipped cream! Not exactly what you'd expect someone to drink on their 21st, but Gabriel's taste buds are a bit different because of the brain damage and he likes what he likes.

Joe came up from Virginia for the celebration, and it marked the first time the whole family had been together since I left for the internship; I thought it'd also be our last. I figured I'd post an Insta pic commemorating the occasion. Maybe that's vain, but we all looked happy, and I wanted them to have that when I was gone.

"They're not gonna understand, you know?" I said to the lightning bug as he continued resting on my hand. He flashed his bulb and I smiled in spite of myself, again wishing I could've just stayed a kid forever. Then none of this would've happened. "It's not their fault, but they'll blame themselves."

I couldn't allow that. They were worried about me, and even that was taking a toll on them. I saw the anxiety and confusion in their faces, especially my Mom's. All kinds of alarm bells and whistles were going off for her, but everything happened so fast, and I constantly lied telling them I was fine. There was nothing for anyone to do. Madison's sister said as much when talking about Madison's depression, "It feels like one day she was happy, the next she was sad, and the day after she was gone." That's what it would feel like for my family too; I had to make sure it didn't destroy them. That's all that mattered, because in my mind, I was already dead.

I stopped avoiding suicide letters. I didn't actually write any, but I thought about them all the time after the camping trip, drafting them in my mind over and over again. They had to be perfect. These letters represented my legacy; I wasn't a builder, but maybe they'd save me from becoming a destroyer of others, especially those I loved.

For Joe, I wanted him to know I was sorry for leaving him. We did everything together. I mean, we've been together since before we were born! But he had Sam now, and it was her job to take care of him going forward. I told him not to worry about me, that I'd be ok, and he would too. I wanted him to know that I looked up to him and considered myself lucky to count him as my twin.

For my Mom – well, I just told her sorry about a million times. After everything with Gabriel, she always told us she'd never make it if anything happened to Joe or me. I needed her to know that wasn't true, that she was strong enough to make it, and that what happened to me wasn't her fault. She was the greatest Mom I ever could've asked for; sometimes these things just happen and there's nothing anybody can do about it.

For my Dad, I wanted him to know I always thought he was a total badass. He was a rock, and I was proud of him. I asked if he was proud of me because I didn't know if he was, or if I was just a disappointment to him. I told him not to become bitter or angry because of what I did. The pain of my death shouldn't drive him to a dark place; he had a lot of life ahead of him, and I wanted him to live it fully.

What to leave Gabriel was trickier. He wouldn't understand a letter. He wouldn't get why I wasn't around anymore either, but I wanted him to know I loved him. I decided I'd get him a stuffed animal, something Dr. Seuss themed because those are his favorite. He saw a Sneetch in a store at Universal Studios when we were little and fell in love. Over the years, we've collected all kinds of Dr. Seuss themed stuffed animals for him, and he sleeps with all two dozen every night. That'd be a perfect gift to leave him.

But I didn't leave him that gift. I didn't leave any gifts, and I didn't write any letters, because in what were supposed to be my final moments, I remembered I had a choice. We all have choices to make – tough ones. Doing what's right, and living *is* right, often leads to pain. It's worth it. You won't be able to see that if you're in the thick of the illness, and you may truly believe you don't have a choice anymore as I did. But I was wrong; we always have a choice.

I chose to live. So can you.

The "Full Circle" Story

The sun shone with the warmth of a pleasant, autumn fire as Erica and I walked to our first-ever college classes. Mine was in Forum building; hers was in Willard, so along the same route, but a bit further down the way. We left earlier than I wanted to, but I liked her and wasn't going to trade the chance to spend time together for ten more minutes of sleep. We strolled down Curtain Ave, chatting about this and that, still getting to know one another. I bounced on the balls of my feet, free, hopeful, buoyed by the overwhelming sense of opportunity radiating from thousands of other students heading to class. The same electricity coursed through my veins the first time I visited Penn State; I belonged here.

I strolled up to the Forum building as the 8am lecture let out and hundreds of students streamed through the doorways back onto campus. Then, I stepped over the precipice and into the auditorium for my first class. I choose a seat on the left side of the room, where I'd sit for the remainder of the semester, and pushed my book bag under my seat. A lanky guy with white-blonde hair sat next to me and introduced himself as Colin. We shook hands, got to talking, and then started shaking hands with everybody around us. We all smiled and laughed like reunited, long-lost friends until the professor settled us down and intro-duced himself.

"My name is doctor John Lear," he said. "Welcome to Chemistry one-ten. Come in, come in. Sit on the stairs if you don't have a seat. It won't be this way for long."

I was glad Erica got me to class early because the audito-rium was packed tighter than a can of sardines. Every seat was taken, and the stairs were filled from the lecture floor to the doorways .Truthfully, I'm not sure how that was even allowed. Maybe the university had a deal with the Fire Marshall – don't check the rooms until *after* the first exam.

How great was this?! I was in college! This was the first day of the rest of my life. There was no telling where the next four years would take me. Even the sky wasn't the limit, and I was so filled with hope, I'm still surprised I didn't burst.

Fast forward four years and I trudged up the path towards Forum for the first class of my final semester. Well, it wasn't my class, it was my friend Brendon's class, but I went with him anyway. He asked me to, and depression haunted me most in the mornings, so I decided it was best to have a reason to get out of bed. Besides, the class was Chemistry 110, same as the first class I ever took at Penn State. I have no idea how Brendon got away with not taking that class as a biology major until his super senior year, but whatever. I decided I'd tag along; full circle and all that, you know?

We arrived at Forum a few minutes before class began and waited outside as the 8am lecture ended. The hallway was stuffed like a Christmas turkey with nervous freshman. Many of them had a dorm-key-lanyard hanging out of their pocket, the sign of a true college newbie. They radiated excitement the same as I did on my first day, but it couldn't reach me as if depression formed a lead shield around me. I felt nothing but bitter disappointment. I was a miserable loser who stood in the same place as four years earlier with nothing to show for it.

It had been two weeks since I got back from New Mexico, and the only reason I was still alive was because I hoped I'd somehow just die so I didn't have to kill myself. I could have a heart attack or an aneurysm or maybe Zeus would launch a lightning bolt from Mt. Olympus to smite me. I didn't care how it happened, I just wanted it to happen so I didn't have to do it. My death would be tragic, but at least my family would never bear the burden of knowing I *wanted* to die. They wouldn't carry the guilt of believing it was their fault.

As the professor performed mad-scientist, first-day experiments to capture the class' attention, I began praying.

Please, God. Please take me. Let my life end. I can't do this, I can't.

I'm sorry. I don't want to pray for this. I don't know what else to do.

I'm begging You. Save me from this. Save my family from this.

Let me die. I'll take someone else's place. Give them my life, I'll take their sickness.

I don't care about the pain. I'll take their pain.

Please, God. Please just let me go. I can't...

Nothing makes you feel like the biggest scumbag on the planet quite like asking the God who gave you a perfect life to take it back. I was so ashamed I'm shocked I didn't pass out from sheer humiliation. Even God must've been disgusted with me for being such a pathetic low life. I figured if I bargained – offered my life for someone else's – then maybe He'd answer my prayer. But the class ticked by, and to my utter disappointment, I kept breathing.

As I looked around the auditorium, I grew angry at those around me for not realizing what I now understood; life was pointless. I was a fool to think attending college mattered, and so were they. What did any of it matter? We like to believe there's purpose to our lives, but we're all running in a damn hamster wheel to nowhere. Why couldn't we admit that truth? Was I the only one with the courage to take the red pill and wake the hell up? The rage built within me like a bomb counting down to explosion. Before it detonated, I cut a wire diffusing my anger and allowed it to seep out of me replaced by a dull sadness.

It wasn't their fault – the pain I experienced. They had nothing to do with it. I refused to allow the bitterness of my depression bring destruction to others. And truthfully, I had nothing to be angry about. I lived a wonderful life, a blessed life full of faith, family, love, and opportunity. This one, horrible experience, this thing that happened to me that I still didn't understand as depression, would not destroy my character. If I was going to go, I'd go as me and not some jerk who lashed out at others on his way out the door.

I don't remember much from the rest of that day. I stumbled through it in a haze, knowing my time was drawing to a close, and drank myself into oblivion that night. Monday may not be your typical day for heavy drinking, but it was Sylly week and I was a super senior drinking with a bunch of other super seniors. That's what we did every night since we got back to school the Wednesday before classes. Six nights of drinking in a row. Then each morning I'd wake up with a hellish hangover motivated only by the thought of dying "naturally," knowing that if I survived the day, I'd be rewarded by drowning my despair in Fireball.

I knew it wouldn't last, and it didn't – depression always found a way to cut off my relief system. Tuesday morning, I woke up violently nauseous. Eating was out of the question. Not that I ate much the previous few days anyway. I typically nibbled on crackers throughout the day, then crammed a slice of pizza down my throat for the sole purpose of drinking without becoming horrifically ill; I made that mistake once freshman year and the memory has been branded into me. But without the ability to eat *anything*, there'd be no drinking.

I told my friends I couldn't make it out that night and took a bunch of much-deserved crap for it because I was always the first to call someone a marshmallow for not going out unless they were sick. Then I laid down on the couch to watch *Friends* hoping the comedy would take the edge off my panic attacks. It didn't. Crushing waves of guilt consumed me, as the all-too-familiar icy adrenaline pumped through my veins. The world around me grew quiet, and I realized I was alone...

Is it time?

Not yet.

I forced my mind to shut down as I moved from the couch to my bed. Maybe if I could sleep without alcohol, the world would be better in the morning. Maybe if I could make it till tomorrow, things would get better.

But making it till tomorrow didn't prove easy. I never fell asleep. Waves and waves of panic attacks ravaged me, each more powerful than the last. Icicles pierced my chest, and the dark of night came alive, wrapping itself around me and choking me like a boa constrictor. My mind dissolved into irrational babbling nonsense, and I thought I might go insane. The pain brought tears to my eyes, and in my head, I wailed in agony as an all-consuming fear of total annihilation swallowed me.

PLEASE! Please, I'm begging You! End this.

Silence.

I can't go on like this! I can't! I'm weak. Please.

Silence.

PLEASE! Please help me! Something. Anything! Please! Please. Please…

More silence. More panic. And so it went all night and I didn't sleep a wink. The price of making it till tomorrow was high, but eventually the merciful sun rose and took the edge off my despair. I sat up in bed feeling like I got run over by a herd of elephants. I was so tired my bones ached, but I made it through the night, and my mind was intact. I hadn't slipped into insanity. This was my last stand; I fought to win.

I'm sick and tired of this!

I'm done! Done feeling this way. Done feeling sorry for myself.

I'm beating this thing! Giving one hundred percent. Everything! All on the field.

No more being a whiny, little bitch!

I'm Lucas-fucking-Wolfe! Let's go!

Yeah, that may have been the vanity talking. As I've said, I had an ego, but that morning my ego might've saved my life. Sure, pride played a role over the years in preventing me from reaching out for help, but in what could've been my final moments, the weapon of mass destruction became a tool for salvation. Go figure.

I needed to eat, so I went to the kitchen and put a Wegman's everything bagel in the toaster. While it toasted, I hopped in the shower the same as I would any other day. I needed to shampoo, wash my body, dry off, get dressed, eat. Those were my objectives to complete before heading to class. They were all I allowed myself to think about. But intrusive thoughts don't care about what you *allow* yourself to think about; the damn bastards push themselves into your head whenever they feel like it.

I saw myself lying in the tub dead, wrists slit.

No! No, no, no, no, no!

I closed my eyes against the gruesome image pressing my palms against them as if trying to push the thoughts out of my head. I needed to shampoo, wash my body, dry off...

Another image exploded in my mind, this one of my stiff, gray body laying in bed after guzzling a bottle of pills. Despite the hot water, I shivered like a featherless penguin in Antarctica.

Wash my body. Eat... Dry off?

No... no.

What... what am I doing?

Brain fog, Category 5 level brain fog, took over my mind. My thoughts crawled to a stop. The haze was as thick as an overgrown jungle, and I hacked away at it just to hear myself think.

Eat. You need to eat.

The thought of food caused me to double over gagging; my whole body seized from the effort. I dropped to my knees, one hand along the wall for support. As I hung my head by the drain, I looked at my body and nearly puked from disgust. My ribs protruded effortlessly, and my stomach was sunken in giving me a skeletal look. I shouldn't have been surprised; I was thin to begin with and lost almost thirty pounds since my internship began. All the same, my physical deterioration shocked me. Most of the time I didn't believe the pain in my head was real, but there was no denying the illness had me looking like I was ready for a gig on *The Walking Dead*.

I knelt in the tub like that until tears stopped sliding down my cheeks. Then I spit a puddle of bile down the drain, got out of the shower, threw some clothes on, and went into the kitchen to eat. I buttered the bagel, then stared at it for a few minutes. This bagel walled off my future; I needed to rehearse getting over it to ensure I had a future. I envisioned taking a bite, chewing, swallowing. Taking another bite, chewing, swallowing.

And after I ate the bagel, I'd grind through the rest of the day. Then the next day and the next day, one step at a time until I climbed out of whatever hellhole I'd fallen in.

But that didn't happen.

The instant the bagel touched my tongue, I gagged. I heaved on the edge of my chair again and again and again the way dogs do before they puke, but nothing came out. So, I attempted a second bite. This time all I did was look at the bagel. I just looked at it, and I started gagging. There was no way I'd be able to eat it. And then I knew; it was over. I made my last stand. I lost. Now, the whistle truly blew. It was time for me to die; there was nothing else for me to do. I left it all on the field. Everything.

Everything? real-me asked.

Everything, depressed-me answered. *There's nothing else. There's no point!*

As depressed-me wailed in despair and another wave of panic washed over me, my real half pushed intrusive thoughts into my mind, only this time they weren't gruesome images of death; they were memories.

My Dad in the snow-covered backyard showing Joe and me how to use our knees to break sticks for the fire. My Mom playing Brain Quest with us as we waited for the school bus. Gabriel holding onto my arm as he stood for the first time smiling from ear to ear. Playing cards in my Mom-mom and Pop-pop's kitchen after a day of Christmas shopping. Joe and I attempting the shortcut on Rainbow Road and laughing our asses off as our characters flew off the map and into La-La Land.

I saw Erica grinning with her squinty eyes from behind the door in 203 Snyder the day we met. Sumit the time he spilled nacho cheese all over himself at a volleyball game. Orto and I teaming up to unlock Bowser in Mario golf. Sam the many times she'd try to be mad at me for being ridiculous, but I'd make her laugh, and it always irritated her that she couldn't stay mad long enough to yell at me.

I saw Luke the time we were all stressed because it was finals week. We took a break to play *Wii Tanks* and I got really far and it was super intense and everyone was yelling encouragement and the screen was so crazy you could barely tell what was going on when all of a sudden the enemy tank blew up and Luke roars, "Yeah! Tell your friends!" and everyone nearly pissed themselves laughing.

I saw my three oldest friends: Seamus, Alex, and Dolan. The day Joe, Seamus, and I made boats out of random crap we found in the woods then tried to sink each other's ships as they made their way down the creek. The time Alex and I ran down a mountain side in Vermont pretending to be in the CIA while everyone else slept from a full day of skiing. The time Dolan and I were the only lifeguards old enough to drive past 11, so our coworkers threw 20's at us as they rushed out of Applebee's to beat curfew, but it was way too much money and we ended up making about $30 each that night.

I saw Matthew and Eric and Sami, technically my cousins but more like brothers and a sister, and the long lazy summers we had at the swim club as kids. I lived such a rich, beautiful life; I couldn't just throw it away.

Don't give up.

I can't do this anymore.

You can.

I can't! There's something wrong with me. I'm broken.

You're strong.

Strong?! Look at yourself? How can you say that?

Because after all these years, you're still here, still fighting.

That's because you're too much of a coward to just end it already.

No, I'm keeping a promise.

Fuck your promise! And fuck you! You ruin everything you touch. Erica, your family – they deserved better.

But you're thinking of them now. You care, and so do they.

It doesn't matter. There's no fixing someone like me. I've tried everything!

Everything?

What more do I have to give?! What else is there to try?

You can call them.

And tell them what?

That you need help.

There is no help for me.

There's always help.

Just let me go. Please... I'm begging you. I'm ready. Just let me go.

I can't.

Please, please just let me die.

You've got more to give, just a little more to give.

I don't! I'm nothing, worthless, a destroyer.

You promised... you promised to be a builder. You are a builder! You are a builder! You– I am a builder!

With that thought in mind, I pushed away from the counter and walked outside to call my Dad and tell him everything.

Recovery:

How Reaching Out Saved My Life

Class let out, and I joined the throngs of students navigating Penn State's labyrinthine sidewalks. Most rushed past me as I meandered along, content to move at my own pace. Fluffy, cotton ball clouds hung low in the sky, and the sun shone with surprising warmth for late October. The air was light and smelled of crisp leaves, most of which had fallen from their trees though a few stragglers still clung to their branches in the hopes of riding out winter.

I stopped to sit on a bench by Old Main; it was a few minutes before the top of the hour, and I wanted to hear the bells ring their full "Fight on State" chimes. Hundreds of people walked by, all of them talking, laughing, smiling, texting. They were headed somewhere, but whether that somewhere was class or the gym or to meet up with friends for lunch, I had no idea. What I did know is that each one of them had dreams. They had hopes. They had struggles and hardships. Some were probably dealing with heartbreak, others with new-found love. Some believed they walked in line with their destiny, others felt lost and adrift. Many of them had it all together, but maybe just as many split apart at the seams. And in a year, maybe those who had it all together would be falling apart and those who were splitting at the seams would have it all together. Who knew? Life's funny like that.

A few months ago, I stood atop a mountain in New Mexico and admitted I wanted my life to end. Now, I sat on a bench in Happy Valley full of hope for what lie ahead content to simply watch people walk by as I waited for a couple of bells to chime.

For years and years and years, I fell down a pit unable to stop my descent into darkness. Then, within a few weeks, I had been plucked out of the fire and given a second chance at life. Sure, I was a smoldering wreck covered in burns and scars, my mind and spirit ravaged by the destruction of depression, my identity razed to nothing. But I was alive. I had hope.

It took a tremendous amount of work to believe in hope again, yet I hardly began to climb the Everest of my recovery. There was a long way to go, and much healing I needed to work through. I'd have to rebuild myself from the ground up. After twenty-two years, I had no idea who I was anymore. I didn't know what I believed in, or in what direction to lead my life. I didn't even know where to start. That's why I reached out for help.

When I called my Dad, I couldn't tell him what was wrong; I didn't know. Neither did he, nor did my Mom. But they weren't hopeless. They picked me up, one of my arms around each of their shoulders, and helped me on a path to healing one step at a time. They got me to a doctor, encouraged me to take medicine, and built a solid foundation for me to stand upon and declare with certainty that life was good and worth living.

As the days passed by, I saw more and more that this was true. People came out of the woodwork to help me, each one selflessly shouldering some piece of the burden that broke me. They dispelled the myth that I was alone, that I was worthless, that I didn't deserve my life, and lent me their hope when I had none of my own. They brought me back to life and showed me purpose existed in everything.

So, I sat on a bench, the warmth of peace filling me, content to wait for the bells to ring.

The "Leap of Faith" Story

I took a seat on the maroon couch in the living-room-turned-office. A small dog jumped up next to me, his front paws resting on my leg as he got closer to give me a sniff. I figured he was used to strangers coming by since he didn't bark, but he still needed to smell me as all dogs do to make sure I was a friend. I guess he approved because a moment later he curled up in my lap looking at me as if to ask why I hadn't pet him yet.

"Gotta be careful with him. That dog made me his bitch," John, whose office I was in for the first time, warned me. I eyed him in the same manner his dog had just eyed me unsure if he was friend or foe. John wasn't exactly what I expected in a therapist. I thought he'd wear slacks and a button-down like a professional. I expected him to speak slowly with an air of false reassurance while making notes on a clipboard and whispering lots of approving noises like, "Hmm-Hmm," and "Ah, I see." I figured he'd want to interrogate my life, reach back into my childhood, find the "source" of my pain, something like that. Just thinking about it made me want to throw up.

But John wasn't anything like what I expected.

He sported track pants that showed off his old-man socks, and his brightly colored running shoes made tie-dye look tame. Small-rimmed glasses rested on the bridge of his nose. A well-kept goatee hugged his face. He exuded warmth and greeted me with a relaxed handshake and a, "Hey, how you doing? Come in, come in!" like I was an exotic dinner guest and not some basket case. John was good at what he did. My distrust melted immediately, like ice dropped in hot tea, but I kept my guard up anyway. Most psychologists seemed like quacks to me, and John's lanky, bird-like movements gave him away as a quack. I don't trust quacks.

"So, dude, tell me about yourself. What's up? Why are we here? What's going on?" John asked in rapid-fire succession.

"I don't know," I answered truthfully. "I was fine and then I just – I just fell apart."

"And when did that happen."

"I guess a few months ago. Beginning of the summer."

"Anything change that would cause you to fall apart?"

"I don't know. I was in New Mexico. That kinda sucked."

John sat upright at this news like a dog perking up when it hears a strange sound. "New Mexico? Damn dude. Why all the way out there?"

"I got an internship."

"Well that's cool. Was it somewhere decent like Albuquerque? Or was it out in bumble-fuck?"

"It was in Silver City."

"Never heard of it."

"That's cus it's in bumble-fuck."

John busted out laughing. "Oh man! That must have sucked. Fuck! Dude…" I didn't know what to make of this guy, but I found myself laughing despite my best effort not to. John was funny, hilarious actually, and he was the only person I've ever met that dropped the f-bomb more than me (seriously, I spent a good amount of time sanitizing my conversations with John throughout this book, and they still have a lot of swearing, but I liked that about him).

"Ok, so we got New Mexico. What happened before that?"

"I don't know," I answered, a hint of frustration in my voice. John didn't push the point. I'm sure most people don't have a great idea of how they got to his office, or they probably wouldn't be there. "I was fine... I was fine."

I stared out the sliding glass door, miserable and hating myself. If only a boulder would fall out of the sky and crush me, then I'd hide under it and be spared this total humiliation.

"Where we at with the feelings?" John asked. "Scale of one to ten."

"I don't know. A nine? Ten?" I shook my head in disgust. "I've had a good life–"

"Doesn't matter," John interrupted. "Depression will screw you sideways no matter who you are, and it'll make you feel like even worse shit if you're not starving and homeless."

"Depression?" How could I be depressed? I still didn't get it. I didn't connect the dots, not even when I wanted to take my life. Suicide wasn't a symptom of depression in my mind; it was a sign of everything wrong with my character.

"Yeah, depression."

"That doesn't make any sense."

"No? Ok, let me ask you something. You thinking of killing yourself?" For a moment I was silent as his words hung between us like smoke from a bomb.

"If a bus ran me over, of the thousand things I'd feel before I died, I think the last would be relief."

"And what would you call that?" John asked, the look in his eyes compassionate, yet firm. He wanted me to say it. He needed me to accept it. There'd be no boo-hoo for Lucas pity-party under his watch. His approach was one of ripping the band-aid off and addressing the heart of the issue. I appreciated that. Never in my life had I felt as weak and fragile as I did sitting in John's office, yet he didn't treat me like I was broken. That mattered.

"I'd call it depression."

John nodded his approval. Then he explained the science of depression and anxiety – another illness I was surprised to learn I struggled with (the feelings of emptiness and thoughts of suicide were mostly driven by depression; the panic attacks and sense of impending doom were mostly driven by anxiety). He told me untreated depression often gave rise to its sister illness, and that the two worked in concert to wreak havoc upon their host's mind.

He talked about chemicals in the brain – serotonin, endorphins, dopamine – all the usual suspects you hear about. He also mentioned cortisol, a chemical released as part of our stress response. It regulates our body's alarm system driving our fight-or-flight instinct. Sometimes that system malfunctions leaving us in a state of perpetual alarm which is why those suffering from anxiety can experience feelings of doom while sitting on the couch eating ice cream.

John continued waving all over the place like an inflatable flailing arm man as he explained the theory behind using medicine and talk therapy to combat mental illness. The medicine was meant to lift the crushing weight of depression. Talk therapy laid out techniques to counter the illnesses' effectiveness. Taken together, these treatments had a success rate approaching 90%. That was good news.

I also liked that there was more to talk therapy than I realized. Before John explained it, I thought it was simply me discussing my feelings with a professional – can't say I was thrilled by that idea. However, therapy proved to be more about catching and redirecting negative thought patterns than it was about expressing feelings. For instance, I believed I was worthless – why? Did I believe everyone was worthless, and if not, why were others worth something while I was worth nothing? That's a double-standard; why did I employ it against myself as a weapon? All it did was bring me pain, and I understood that, yet I continued my destructive behavior. Why? Did I believe I deserved to be in pain? Why did I deserve to be in pain? Because I was worthless?

Here, John pointed out my logic was circular and therefore illogical. The root of the thought pattern driving my sense of worthlessness went deeper. Until we uncovered it, we couldn't redirect it and my depression would stay stuck at the high end of the scale.

When I was younger, I used to think this kind of thing was a bunch of cockamamie bullcrap. Sitting in John's office, I still thought it was bullcrap until he pointed out I did things my way my whole life which ultimately landed me in his office.

"You think maybe it's time to let someone else steer the ship?" he asked.

"Yeah I guess so."

"You're gonna have to let me in. You think you're Superman, so I know you don't like to do that."

"I will."

"Will you?"

"I don't even know how I got here. I won't find my way back, not on my own. So yeah, I'll let you in, I'll let you steer. I'll take that leap of faith. It's all I have."

The "It's Possible" Story

When I ran track in high school, I had the goal of running a sub 5-minute mile. Not an easy feat, but not that difficult when you run every day either, and I achieved it within a year. I still remember seeing the clock read 4:55 as I crossed the finish line before stumbling to a nearby trashcan in case I puked. I was thrilled to be a part of the sub-5 club, but my body felt like it got run over by a truck. Everything hurt. My legs wobbled. My stomach was a brick. I couldn't catch my breath and my head throbbed. The toll was enormous. I couldn't imagine possibly running any faster, yet plenty of people did all the time. Some even ran a mile in under 4 minutes!

Roger Bannister, an Englishman, was the first to do so. Before 1954, the year he smashed through that elusive barrier, scientists believed it was impossible for humans to run a sub-4 mile. Not difficult. Not really, really hard. Impossible. And why wouldn't they? People tried running under 4 minutes for thousands of years. The ancient Greeks called it *paideia*, or perfection. They're rumored to have taken drastic measures pursuing paideia, such as tying themselves to horse-drawn chariots, or even unleashing lions to chase the runners. But none succeeded, and we accepted the challenge as impossible.

Until Roger Bannister.

When asked how he accomplished a feat that escaped humanity's capability for thousands of years, Roger said he envisioned it in his mind; he saw himself crossing the finish line at 3:59 again, and again, and again. He believed it was possible, and so it was.

In the three years after Roger broke that infamous barrier, sixteen others broke it as well. That's impressive! But not as impressive as the fact that in the next fifty plus years, hundreds and hundreds of people joined the sub-4 club, including high school kids. How? How did no one break this record for thousands of years, and then hundreds of people did one after the other in a little over fifty? What changed? They knew it had been done. They believed it was possible and had faith that if someone else could do it, so could they (I got this Roger Bannister story from a speech made by Les Brown).

I needed to have that same faith if I was going to beat depression. I needed to believe it was possible, but I didn't. John could see that in me; he could see in my eyes that I had given up. Even as I promised him I'd take the leap, I thought nothing would come of it. He had to change my mind about that, and he was desperate to do so.

"I need you to feel the relief," John said as he secured a prescription for Klonopin, an anti-anxiety medicine, towards the end of our first meeting. "You're hurting, and we've gotta make sure you see the light." He went on to explain that Klonopin was a fast-acting medicine used in the short-term to help people sleep. It was also used as an emergency medicine to combat panic attacks because your mind melts a little during those assaults making people vulnerable to impulsively taking their life.

"We're also gonna use Zoloft. Tighten this thing up," John continued. He used "we" a lot. "We'll get better. We'll get through this. We'll be ok." He did this to break through the isolation of depression, one of the most effective methods of treating the illness. It's easier to hold on when you've got something to hold onto. And I needed that because Zoloft works like a vitamin meaning it takes about eight weeks to really kick in. I didn't have that kind of time.

Imagine you had a headache that wouldn't quit. You tried and tried and tried to ease the pain it caused you, but nothing worked; it only ever got worse. Over the course of many months and years, the headache dismantled you piece by piece until you were crippled – unable to eat, unable to sleep, unable to enjoy anything in life because of the torment. Then someone comes along and offers you a pill you're afraid to take. You've heard horrible things about this medicine. People call it poison. They say it disturbs your mind. Movies and tv shows portray anyone who takes it as either turning into a zombie or a crazed lunatic who needs to be tased anytime he breaks free of his straight jacket. Then you're told these same meds might maybe start to cure your headache in two months. Not exactly much of a solution.

That's where the Klonopin comes in. I was just as afraid to take that as the anti-depressant (Zoloft), but at least it worked within an hour. If I lost my mind, it'd go quickly. Always have to look for that silver lining!

I picked up the meds on my way home from John's office, then sat at my kitchen table staring at them wondering how these little, circular pills would do anything to help. My parents hung around in case I needed encouragement but kept a healthy distance so as not to hover over me. I was their broken child; I can't imagine how much they wanted to rush in and fix me, to take my pain away. But they couldn't, so they waited. Finally, I popped the pill and washed it down with a gulp of water. I was immediately overcome by a torrent of emotions; sadness, rage, guilt, humiliation. Fighting back tears, I walked over to my Dad and asked for a hug. He looked confused – he's not much of a hugger and neither am I – but didn't question it.

"Dad…" I said blubbering on his shoulder like a baby.

"Yeah?"

"I'm such a bitch." We both started laughing, and it took a while for us to stop. I was supposed to be at Penn State hanging with my friends, not crying on my Dad's shoulder at 22-years-old. I was supposed to be finishing my last semester of college, not seeing a therapist for depression and anxiety. I was supposed to be invincible, but I was broken. I guess there's nothing to do but cry a bit when you realize all of that.

About an hour later though, the strangest thing happened; I felt normal! Not depressed, not anxious – normal. I wasn't high. I didn't turn into a zombie. I wasn't crazy. I just felt normal like depression had been sucked right out of me. The sludge in my mind cleared like fog lifting when the sun shines after a storm. The lead in my bones dissolved giving me an airy and light feeling as if I'd float up to the clouds and bounce from one to the other. I wanted to fly through the sky, let the world know I was free! They could be free too!

Then the medicine began wearing off. Slowly, it receded like the tide returning to the sea, and the pain of depression took its place. I longed for another pill to feel normal again because I forgot how wonderfully amazing it is to feel normal, but I wasn't allowed to take another, not yet. Back to Hell for me for the time being, and the fires were just as hot, but I stood a little taller. The memory of relief gave me strength like a lifeboat approaching a drowning swimmer.

The medicine worked! I thought I was gone; that it was impossible for me to come back, impossible to fix me. I didn't believe medicine could even touch the sickness that ailed me, yet it won me my first true breath of freedom. I had hope again. Hope that the medicine would work. Hope that talk therapy would work. Hope that I could get better.

I believed it was possible because I felt the relief, and having that faith changed everything.

The "One Hour Rule" Story

My legs carried me up the grassy hill as I kept stride with the front of the pack. My heart thumped against my ribs, its beat calm and consistent. My body weighed as much as a feather unimpeded by its usual buildup of lactic acid. Deep breaths filled my lungs. Ahead, I saw the clock marking time for the first mile. I snuck a peak as I ran past; 5:05!

Holy shit! I can't keep this up.

Only a few months prior, I broke 5 minutes for the first time. Now, I nearly did it again except this was a cross country race; I still had 2.2 miles to go! When I set that personal record, I stumbled around half dead with jelly legs afterwards. I couldn't even jog my warm down. How was I supposed to finish another two miles?

My heartbeat wasn't so calm anymore. It pounded against my ribs, and I was afraid it might burst (I heard about that kind of thing happening to horses when they raced; I didn't know if it could happen to humans, but I didn't want to find out). My limbs turned to concrete. My breaths became shallow. The pack pulled ahead, and people passed me like wildebeests overrunning Simba; I made no move to catch them. Eventually, I staggered across the finish line.

"What happened?" my coach demanded. "You fell off!"

"I don't know. I saw my mile time–"

"And you didn't think you could keep it up?"

"Yeah."

"We talked about this–"

"I know!"

"A hundred meters at a time."

"How?"

"How what?"

"How do I forget about the other two miles!"

"Practice! You practice, and then you just do it."

He wasn't wrong. Disciplining our minds doesn't require magic, just practice, the same as honing a physical skill. It's more difficult – our thoughts are unruly, and our minds wander like curious toddlers – but it's not impossible. I learned how to set boundaries when I ran so I only tackled 100 meters at a time; now I needed to learn how to set them so I only lived an hour at a time. That's unfortunately as much as I could handle. All I wanted was to punch my ticket and call it a life. There was too much to do every day, and I didn't want to face it all.

First, I'd wake up and have to get out of bed, which was impossible. How anybody found the strength to get up and face the eternally unending day was beyond me. I used to spring out of bed like SpongeBob when he had a shift at the Krusty Krab, but that was a version of myself from a past life. Now, it took all my strength just to sit up against the wall.

After that, I'd have to shower. The meds made me sweat in my sleep like I broke a fever, so there was no skipping this task. Showering presented me with a few problems one of which was the number of steps involved. Turn the water on, stand in the tub, shampoo, wash my body, dry off – impossible. The second problem was the significance of a shower. It indicated a willingness to take on the day, to be a part of the world. I wanted neither of those things, and my mind rebelled like a desperate hostage. My depressed half tormented me, and it was exhausting to fight him over every little thing. By the time I wrapped the towel around my waist, I'd be ready for bed. But I couldn't go to bed. There was more to do.

I had to put on deodorant, brush my teeth, comb my hair, get dressed (another task involving a stupid number of steps), make breakfast, eat breakfast. Then I'd walk to class, take notes, pack my books up, go to the next class, study…

I'd have to make lunch, then dinner. I had to remember to take my anti-depressant in the morning, unless I couldn't eat breakfast, then I'd have to take it after lunch. But if I couldn't stomach breakfast, I'd be anxious about lunch. What if I couldn't eat either meal? I'd be screwed because I needed to eat to take the medicine. But even if I choked down lunch, would it matter? Would the meds work as intended if I didn't take them at the same time every day? Thinking about that sent my anxiety through the roof. On top of all this crap hanging over my head, I still worried about homework and grades. How would I pass my classes when I was plagued by perpetual brain fog and didn't have the strength to get up in the morning? Better to stay in bed.

John wasn't surprised to hear about these fears of survivability even though it took him some time to yank the truth out of me. I didn't want to admit it; I felt like a loser. I used to be able to handle anything. When others dropped from exhaustion, I kept pushing like an energizer bunny on crack. I didn't need coffee or Red Bull or Adderall; I had my pride, that was enough. Now I had nothing, and a single day was more than I could bear. So, John shrunk the window of life to one hour. That's it, that's all I was allowed to focus on. I couldn't worry about dinner as I made breakfast. I couldn't worry about an exam a week away when I had to put on my shoes to get to class. Once an hour was finished, I let it go and moved on to the next one.

Every morning began the same with me blearily opening my eyes like I woke from hibernation. The dream I left felt as if it still happened around me, so I'd let my alarm buzz pulling me into reality. It was nice to be able to sleep again – John said tightening up my sleep was his number one priority – but the meds gave me crazy dreams. I mean *way* crazy. And vivid. They were so real that waking up felt more like a dream and the dream more like reality. Either way it sucked because reality was accompanied by the bitter disappointment that I was still alive.

Why can't I just die in my sleep?
Get up Lucas.
I can't.
You can.
What's the point?
Just get up.
No! There's nothing. It's useless.
It's not.
You should've killed yourself when you had the chance.
Well I didn't.

156

I'd throw my legs over the side of the bed and drag my ass to the shower. I always made it hot because hot showers are relaxing. As the water washed over me, I'd lean against the wall imagining depression flowing out of me to rush down the drain with the rest of the dirt. Sometimes I'd stand like that for half an hour. Sometimes even longer. It was one of the ways I was kind to myself, another skill John charged me with learning.

"You got this hammer thing down," he told me in one early session. "You're a blunt instrument. You've got no moderation, no finesse. You're all grit."

"Isn't grit good?"

"Sure, but not when you do it stupid!" John busted out laughing. I just looked at him unsure if I should be pissed about what he said or accept it.

"Look," he continued, "I'm not trying to be hard on you. You're a strong guy, I admire that about you, but you beat yourself up over everything. Have the strength to be kind to yourself."

So, in the beginning, those were the two weapons I wielded against depression; the one-hour rule and kindness towards myself (I still throw up in my mouth a bit when I say that but whatever it worked). It wasn't easy. We're built to move towards the future, but one hour wasn't much of a future. My mind constantly wandered past its boundaries, driven by anxiety and depression, and I'd have to smack it back in line.

I trained my thoughts in the same way you'd train a puppy to wait for the "Ok" before eating. Put a bowl of food in front of a puppy, and he darts at it like a wild animal. You've got to grab him and pull him back telling him no. The second you let go, he dives at the food again. Pull him back, tell him no. He dives. Pull him back, tell him no. He'll whimper. He'll whine. He'll look cute as a button to tug on your heartstrings, but you wait him out anyway. You're the boss, and the puppy has to learn that. So did my thoughts. Sure, they had a degree of free-dom to roam around on their own, the same as you'd give a puppy, but there were rules. If my thoughts broke the rules, I'd smack them back in line. Without John's help, I wouldn't have learned to do this nor would I have understood the value of treating myself with kindness when I inevitably failed again and again and again to stick to the one-hour rule.

My normal response would've been to beat up on myself for being pathetic and weak feeding my sense of worthlessness. John taught me I was worth being kind to. Weird, because you'd think we would believe that about ourselves, or that it'd be easy to accept if we didn't; it's not. It's painful. It's easier to hate ourselves than treat ourselves with dignity. I haven't fully worked out why that's true, but I know from experience that it is.

At any rate, the kindness thing proved I had to change. I couldn't be the same person who drove me to thoughts of sui-cide and expect to get better, a fact John reminded me of often.

"Look where you're sitting," he'd say whenever I stub-bornly battled him. "You're in my office. You think maybe you fucked up somewhere along the way, Superman?"

Whenever John said this, I'd laugh a little and shrug my shoulders as if to say, "I guess so." He was right; of course I screwed up! My thought patterns were destructive and un-healthy despite my intention of being strong and self-reliant. I built most of my identity on the fig leaf of hubristic pride and held myself to an impossible standard. That had to change. I had to change, and here's the unpopular conclusion born from that realization; I wasn't perfect the way I was. Neither are you.

The idea of being perfect the way we are comes from a good place. It comes from compassionate people who had the heart and the wisdom to understand that not everyone had to fit per-fectly into a predetermined mold to have value. The so-called "misfits" had as much worth as anyone else, hence, "you're perfect just the way you are." In that sense, the saying is absolutely correct. Unfortunately, it's been hijacked by unserious narcissists who love snarky memes like, "If they can't handle you at your worst, they don't deserve you at your best." Uh, maybe, but maybe our worst is totally unacceptable and instead of being an ass about it we should attempt to improve ourselves.

That is a *bitter* pill to swallow. We do not like to change and the reasons for that are many and multi-faceted. I have no intention of going down that rabbit hole here, so I'll leave it at this; you are worth changing for. Have the courage and humility required to accept our need for change, and to believe you're worthy of the better, more joy-filled life that waits for you on the other side of it.

I tried to accept that fact when I got back to school after spending a few days at home. During that time, I met John, picked up my meds, and got my feet back under me somewhat. John wanted me to take the semester off, but I told him I thought that would make things worse for me; to my surprise he didn't push back and agreed to hold our sessions over Skype so I could stay at college.

For the next two weeks, I did my best to stick to the one-hour rule. I'd wake up in a delirious haze, then spend some time lying in bed wishing I died in my sleep and battling my depressed half. Eventually, I'd force myself up to get a shower. Sometimes that'd bring on a panic attack because taking a shower meant I planned on making it through the day; other times I successfully walled off the future keeping my mind within the bounds of a single hour.

I'd go to class, fighting my demons the entire time, then head to the gym for a light workout. The exercise was healthy, but it terrified me. What if it sapped too much of my energy and I didn't have enough left over to battle depression? Remember,

I needed a minimum level of energy to keep depression at bay. If the fear became too much, I'd forgo the gym in favor of laying on the couch in my apartment. There, I'd try and decide between ignoring the hollowness in my soul or allowing myself to feel it in the hopes that it'd move on. These battles were typically complemented by more panic attacks. I was supposed to take the Klonopin during situations like this, but I wasn't fully on board with the meds two weeks into treatment, so I suffered through em' like a blockhead.

The rest of my day was filled depending on what I felt up to. Some days I'd work on homework for a bit. Other days I'd go for a walk. Some days I'd apply for jobs, and others I stayed on the couch watching Brendon play Call of Duty. None of it was easy or peaceful, and throughout all of it, images of my suicide assaulted me if I wasn't actively thinking of taking my life. Sometimes I wished I could simply cease to exist; I wished I never was and never would be. Those are destructive thoughts though, and I did my best to push them out of my head.

Then, one morning when my alarm went off, I rolled over and silenced it. I don't remember if the day was cloudy or sunny, only that it was bright, and I blinked a few times as my eyes adjusted to the light. I stood up and stretched with a full body yawn, then grabbed my towel and shuffled to the bathroom. My hair stood up every which way, making me laugh when I looked at my reflection in the mirror. I hopped in the shower allowing the warm water to flatten my hair while thinking of breakfast to gauge my ability to eat. I didn't gag, which was good.

After drying off, I threw some clothes on and fired up the stove. I cracked an egg in the pan, threw a bagel in the toaster, and hummed a tune to myself. A few minutes later I had a slightly overcooked egg covered with a piece of cheese sitting between two halves of an everything bagel. It was delicious.

When I finished eating, I sat at the kitchen bar reading politics on my phone and sipping on a glass of apple juice (what a weird combination of an old-man activity while enjoying a 5-year-old's drink). There was a lot going on at the time leading up to the 2016 election, and even though I hadn't stayed up to date because depression killed my interest in everything, that morning I felt like catching up.

Then I brushed my teeth, packed my books for class, and sat on the edge of the bed to put on my shoes. As I put on the first one, I had the strangest feeling I forgot something. I figured it'd come to me in the middle of the night when, out of nowhere, it hit me like a face full of bricks; I hadn't thought of killing myself yet! When I woke up, I didn't wish I was dead, I just... woke up. No panic attacks, no thoughts of suicide, no despair. I was getting better.

Hope overwhelmed me, and once again tears streamed down my cheeks, but this time from happiness. It's hard to put into words how significant this moment was. Imagine being a prisoner of your own mind, losing control of your thoughts so they tormented you with ideas of death and destruction. Every second of every minute of every day was filled to the brim with empty pointlessness, and despair poisoned your heart for so long you didn't remember life without it. Fear haunted your every waking moment so totally you couldn't believe it hadn't killed you. For years, you fought against this slow death, but eventually you accepted that dying was your only escape. When you reached out for help, it wasn't to save yourself; it was so those who loved you could move on when you died knowing everything that could've been done for you was. Yet that help, the help you didn't believe in, began pulling you out of the darkness.

It wasn't the light at the end of the tunnel, it was only a small ray of light within the tunnel, but that was enough. I had hope again.

The "Birthday Blues" Story

"You always want to learn the hard way," my Dad used to say to me. I heard that so often as a kid, I remember it more as an omnipotent theme echoing throughout the years of my child-hood than as a specific instance. I never seemed to learn from other people's experiences or wisdom, and depression was no different. John told me I needed to change if I truly wanted to get better, but I started getting better without changing. The medicine lifted the pain of despair, so why do anything differ-ent? Why not just let the meds do their thing until I was right as rain? I liked who I was and didn't want to change until I acci-dentally threw myself back into depression. Then I realized the medicine was only ever a temporary reprieve, a crutch to get through the worst of the illness, but not the end-all to solving it. I had to embrace therapy, and train myself to think differently; I had to change.

On my 23rd birthday, I learned this lesson the hard way.

It should've been a great day. For a while, it looked like Joe and I might not have been able to spend that birthday together because it fell on a Wednesday, and I was at school while he worked in Virginia. Then Capital One asked him to represent the company at Penn State's career fair which happened to fall on – you guessed it – our birthday. What a stroke of luck! Joe and I were ecstatic to continue our streak of celebrating to-gether. The only part that sucked? Going to the career fair.

Applying for jobs meant looking into the future, but I was supposed to follow the one-hour rule. John and I came up with that rule, not because I thought it'd be fun to live that way, but because it was all I could handle. Literally. Sometimes people think I'm exaggerating on this point for effect, but I'm not. When you're at rock bottom of a mental health crisis, the conventional "rules" of life go out the window. There's no unlimited willpower to muscle through pain; will is built on strength of identity, but you don't know who you are anymore. You have no endurance to bear the suffering because you have no reason to. If life is pointless, which I believed in my suicidal depression, why suffer? It's all for nothing anyway. You can't simply *will* your way past that dilemma when your spirit, the part of us that drives willpower, is broken.

Think of it like a car. If I asked you to drive a hundred miles, you'd be able to do that easily in under two hours with a decent engine. Now imagine I took the engine out, blew it up, and asked you to drive that same car a hundred miles. You'd look at me like I was insane! You'd be so dumbfounded by how stupid my request was you probably wouldn't even know how to respond. Even if you pushed and shoved and heaved with all your strength all day long, you'd be lucky if the car rolled a mile let alone a hundred. That's what it's like living with suicidal depression. My engine, my spirit, was blown to bits. I couldn't make it a full day at a time. Even the fuel to last an hour came from some part of me I didn't know I had. But talk therapy helps us rebuild our spirit, and the price we pay is letting go of our old self. I wasn't prepared to do that yet, even when John warned me there'd be a steep price to pay if I didn't. So, I threw the one-hour rule in the trash, put on a suit, and headed to the career fair.

"Hey, man what's up?" I said to Joe as I walked over to his booth.

"Not much dude. Weird to be on this side of things."

"Yeah, no kidding."

"How're you doing? You good?" There was a pitch to his voice when he spoke, and I knew he meant about the depression.

"Doing a lot better," I lied. "You know me, I don't stay down for long."

"Good, good. And how's this thing been?"

"Eh, who knows? Some of these people rejected me three years in a row. We'll see if I can go for four."

"It'll work out."

We chatted a bit more, and then Luke, who was with Joe representing Capital One, came over to say hello. The three of us made plans to meet up after the fair, then I left them so they could get back to talking with students. Besides, I had jobs to apply to.

I studied the map of booths sprawling throughout the BJC looking for companies that interested me, but none of them did. Nothing interested me. I pushed those thoughts out of my head and waited in line at a chemical company called Albemarle. They did neat stuff that used to interest me; maybe if I got better, I'd enjoy working there.

The guy behind the booth was as tall as a giraffe, but he had a baby face, which gave him the look of an oversized kid. As I approached him, I pasted a fake smile on my face allowing the mask of my old self to slip over the depression. I had to be on my game. Entertaining, talkative, bright. No one wanted to hire a gloomy, down-in-the-dumps, negative Nellie.

He looked at my resumé for all of five seconds, then said, "Your GPA's not high enough." He made a move to hand it back to me, then thought better of it, placing the worthless summary of my life on the table behind him as if he wouldn't throw it in the trash the minute I walked away. I wanted to be mad, but I wasn't. I dropped the smile, let the mask fall off, and walked to the next booth.

For hours I meandered about hopping from booth to booth like a bee hopping from flower to flower. I carried a paper towel around with me to wipe the beads of sweat that broke out on my forehead – it was unbearably hot in the BJC especially in a suit – and I felt my face droop from exhaustion like melted cheese from a mozzarella stick. Fighting depression drained me of energy. So did the anti-depressants. Drowsiness, and I'd say extreme drowsiness when you first start taking them, is a common side effect. I shouldn't have been at the fair for hours; it was more than I could handle, but I didn't want to admit that. I was supposed to approach the future one tentative step at a time. Instead, I plunged headlong into the task of finding a for-life job, as if jobs are for life, entirely ignoring depression's ability to screw with my head.

Now if I spoke with John about the fair, which I should have since I Skyped with him twice a week, he could've anticipated how depression and anxiety would've messed with me. He would've known I'd push myself past the limit because I hadn't accepted my brokenness yet and found a way to minimize the damage. But I didn't talk to him about it. I knew he'd suggest something like showing up towards the end of the fair so there'd automatically be a limit to the amount of time I spent there. Eff that! Maybe if I got a job offer, I'd prove to myself I wasn't such a worthless loser. Maybe an offer would be a giant step towards fixing myself. Wouldn't overdoing it be worth risking that reward? No, no it wasn't.

As my energy waned, depression moved in for the knockout punch. Hundreds of people scurried about like worker ants possessed by their queen, all of them dressed to the nines carrying official binders and folders filled with embellished resumés. None of them noticed my despair. They didn't understand we were nothing but cogs in a hopelessly infinite machine. Dread overwhelmed me, and I wished with all my heart to be free from the absurdity of life. What was the point? Was this all there was to the world? We're born to slog through school to find a job to slave away for some soulless corporation until retirement which is nothing more than waiting to die. What a useless joke life is! It was cruel for God to have ever made us.

You're going off the deep end buddy. This isn't you.

It is now. I was stupid before.

No, you weren't. Gotta fight that.

Why?

Because it's right.

Nothing's right.

Stop it. You're being a bitch.

I had a rule about feeling sorry for myself which was that I wasn't allowed to. I had a great life; I didn't earn the right to whine about the one awful thing that happened to me. And it wasn't practical. No one ever got better by feeling sorry for themselves. So, I decided to knock it off and exercise a bit to clear my mind. I walked home, changed out of my suit, headed to the gym, and began pumping iron. All through the workout I suffered intermittent panic attacks, but I refused to back down. I refused to take the Klonopin. That was for weaklings. I was strong. I had to be if I wanted to conquer depression (Duh).

On my way back to the apartment, I stopped by a campus computer lab and applied to jobs listed on the school website. After that, I started some homework for my fuels class, then studied a bit for another bio-chemical engineering class I took. My grades were surprisingly decent so far that semester, so I didn't *have* to study at that moment, but the idea was to over-load myself. Maybe if I pushed and pushed and pushed, I'd push the awful thoughts right out of my head. That wouldn't have been such a dumb idea if it weren't the same "coping" strategy I employed for years. It never worked. I needed rest, and I needed to give myself permission to rest, but I wasn't there yet.

Later in the day, I met up with Joe and a few other friends at the apartment to celebrate our birthday. I was totally exhausted and in no mood to drink but took a few shots anyway. That got me in the mood (sometimes, when you're not feeling it, you've gotta do a little of what you're not feeling just to feel it, right?). And holy crap did I get hammered! John warned me I'd get drunk faster while taking anti-depressants because the enzyme that breaks down alcohol also breaks down the medicine. If it was occupied with the meds, it couldn't metabolize alcohol, which got me drunk quicker and kept me drunk longer I saved money at the bars, though. That was cool.

It was a great night! As per birthday tradition, we went to the Phyrst, played pass the pitcher, ate Phyrst fries, shot pool, sang with the band – all the usual stuff. I felt amazing. I knew it was the alcohol, but I didn't care. I was happy that Joe and I got to spend our birthday together. I was happy to leave behind my woes from earlier in the day. I was happy to have one night free from the madness of depression, even if it was only because I was drunk.

But the next morning, I learned why you're not supposed to drink while in the throes of the illness. Never in my life had the phrase, "What fresh hell is this?" been so applicable. The hangover was brutal, breathing new life into my depression like gas poured on a fire. I curled into a tight ball on the corner of my bed, forehead pressed against my knees, arms clasped over my head in an effort to block out the thoughts of destruction.

Please, God! Please take me. Please, I can't. I can't...

Quiet sobs wracked my ravaged body as the sheer magnitude of my brokenness overwhelmed me. I didn't fight them. I didn't have the energy too. Eventually the worst of it passed, and I got up to face the day. I don't remember much of it thanks to brain fog. I do know Erica called in the afternoon to wish me a happy birthday (we were still together in secret). Hearing her voice should've made me happy, but I felt nothing. She sounded cheery, and that made me want to throw my phone at the wall so it'd explode into a million pieces because what the damn hell was there to be cheery about? After our call, I stood in my bedroom alone until a voice pulled me out of some distant corner of my mind like an alarm pulling me out of a dream.

"You ok?" Joe asked. He stood next to me in the bedroom while I stared blankly at the wall. *When did he get here?*

"Fine," I mumbled.

"You sure?"

"I said I'm fine!"

"Well... I've been standing here for... a while. You didn't even notice me." He sounded concerned, but more than that, afraid. He didn't know how bad things really were. None of my family did because I wasn't honest with them. I didn't want them to know how badly I ached for my life to end. They didn't deserve to shoulder that burden, so I hid it from them. I did my best to convince them my battle with depression was nothing more than a temporary inconvenience. They knew I downplayed it, but never would've guessed the happy-go-lucky Lucas they knew wished he were dead. As time went on though, more and more fissures appeared in my crafted façade, and glimpses of the truth leaked out like water seeping through cracked ice.

I tried to say something back, to explain why I hadn't noticed him standing next to me, but no words came out of my flapping mouth. Rage exploded within me like an erupting volcano. I wanted to fling myself at Joe and pummel him to a pulp. All the anger, resentment, and pain would pour out of me as I tore into him with my fists. He deserved it! Who did he think he was asking me if I was ok like he had it all together? Who the hell was he to judge me!

Let it go, Lucas.

He deserves it!
No, he doesn't.
Yes he does! So do you!
You've gotta let go.
You let go! Let go of your life! It's nothing!
It's not nothing to Joe.
Joe's nothing! I hate him!
You love him. You love Erica. You love them all.

My depressed half grew hysterical as he sensed his grip over my mind unravel. I longed to give into the anger – it felt better than the total anguish of depression – but I let it go instead. I chose to let it go. We always have a choice. In that moment, I chose to let my pride die rather than beat my twin to smithereens.

"Joe..." I whispered, tears flooding out of my eyes. "Joe what happened to me? What happened?" He turned to shut the door so no one saw me cry, then caught me as my legs buckled helping me to sit on the bed.

"It's alright man. It's alright. It's just – you're going through a thing," he answered, his ears turning a shade of red.

"It's not alright."

"Well, um, what's – uh what's wrong?"

"I just told you I don't know."

"Oh yeah." The tips of his ears were nearly purple with embarrassment, while the rest of his face turned beet red as he floundered trying to find the right words.

"What the hell is your face red for?" I asked, my head still resting on his shoulder. "I'm the one crying like a bitch."

Joe laughed. "Dude, you're not a bitch. *I'm* the bitch. Look at my ears! They're fucking red, aren't they? I can feel it."

"Yeah, they are. You're right, you're the bitch."

"Seriously. I had to do a presentation the other day. My voice cracked. My ears were red as shit. I almost died." Joe can't speak in front of people to save his life, and it doesn't help any that his voice cracks all the time like he's a prepubescent child. Thinking of him nearly piss himself in front of a room full of people had me laughing my ass off. When I caught my breath, Joe asked me more about depression and I told him the illness "fried my brain." Sometimes I just felt like absolute garbage and there was nothing I could do about it. He looked puzzled, then asked why I hadn't taken the Klonopin. I told him I didn't take it because I felt stupid needing it. He told me I was stupid for thinking that. I agreed, then took the medicine. About an hour later it kicked in and the worst of the depression left me.

The strange thing was, when the medicine wore off, I didn't fall back into the deepest, darkest pit of my illness. I was hurting for sure, but on a scale of one to ten, I'd say I was at an eight which is a heck of a lot better than a nine or a ten. That's the chemistry. That's the whole point of the medicine. My depression and anxiety had gone untreated for so long that the balance of chemicals in my brain was way out of whack. Taking medicine, while actively working on what I learned in therapy to positively affect my brain chemistry, would return me to a healthy level. Suffering through panic attacks like a blockhead didn't make me strong; it simply meant I valued pride more than myself. On my 23rd birthday, in the midst of the birthday blues, the choice between my life and my pride was thrown into stark contrast.

We all have demons that we battle; pride was mine and God knows I've got more. You've got demons too. You know which one threatens to destroy you, just as I did. Pride may not have been the cause of my depression, but it did prevent me from reaching out for help, and that vice almost cost me my life. Don't make the same mistakes I did. Have the courage to face your demons, to admit they exist. None of us are perfect, and we don't have to be. Having faults is part of being human. Face them. Admit them. Own them. Then let them go and learn who you are without them because it may save your life, and at the very least, you'll live a better one.

The "Side Effects" Story

"I know what your spirit animal is," Erica said as her and Sam applied mascara together in the bathroom mirror.

"Yeah, duh, everyone knows my spirit animal," I answered. *My last name is Wolfe, it's pretty obvious.*

"You're a skunk!"

"*What?!* A skunk? Why the hell am I a skunk?"

"Because you fart a lot and it's smelly!" I heard a loud thud from the other room as Joe collapsed on the floor cracking up. "Dude, BURN! She got you so good."

"Yeah she did," Sam chimed in.

"Thanks guys. I made a good joke," Erica declared sticking her tongue out at me. Erica's known for her awful jokes, so anytime she makes a decent one she feels the need to announce it.

It's true though; I farted all the time and these weren't dainty, "Hmm, what's that smell?" farts, these were full-blown rotten egg and sour milk bombs. But that wasn't even the bad part. No, the bad part was I had a too-many-laxative-pills New Mexico style event just about every day, except I never took laxatives, so what the hell?

I thought about going to the doctor. There had to be an explanation, and I couldn't walk around like a ready-to-erupt volcano about to spew brown lava forever. But, before I spoke to anyone about my digestive issues, I messed around with my diet to see if I could figure out the problem myself and surprisingly succeeded. Apparently, I couldn't drink milk.

That didn't make sense. I loved milk! Drank it my entire life and never had a problem. I heard about people developing lactose intolerance as they got older, but I could still eat ice cream and cheese without an issue... or so I thought. Then one fateful day I had an egg sandwich with cheese for breakfast, yogurt as a snack, and a cheesesteak for lunch. That was pretty much the equivalent of setting off a bomb in my stomach. Ouch. Turns out it wasn't just milk that caused the volcano to erupt; too much dairy did the trick as well. But why? I thought back to when these issues began in September around the start of my final semester at Penn State. What changed that may have caused this digestive misfortune? It wasn't hard to figure out; that's when I started taking the medicine.

Yupp, Zoloft gave me the shits; only if I had too much dairy though. So, I cut back a bit and switched to lactose free milk and everything was good after that. I don't get how that works, but whatever. Problem solved. That's all I really cared about. John, however, was a bit more concerned when I told him what I discovered.

"Dude, you should've told me. We could've switched you to something else."

"I didn't want to switch to something else."

"Why not?"

"The Zoloft was working."

"Other meds work too. You don't have to settle for less than the best."

"I wasn't settling." John simply raised his eyebrows asking for an explanation. "Dude, I thought my life was over. Then you offered me a way out and I'm... what? Supposed to complain because it makes me fart if I drink milk?"

"No, no. Not complain," he said dancing around in his leather chair like a cartoon character. "But if it became unbearable, we could talk about it. You don't have to suffer."

"I was suffering. I'm not anymore. I didn't settle, I'm just grateful."

And that's the thing of it; I was grateful. I see so much whining and moping and incessant complaining about the side-effects of psychiatric medicine and I lose my damn mind over it. Do some of the side effects legitimately suck? Yes, absolutely. And John was right about not settling, and not suffering. But there's a difference between not settling, and being a whiny, self-absorbed asshat. For instance, I had a friend who experienced severe, flu-like symptoms when she began taking anti-anxiety medicine. After a month of feeling like she got run over by a truck, she reached out to her doctor and they switched to something else. That's reasonable. But when someone writes a snarky article titled, "What They *Don't* Tell You About Anti-Depressants" featuring complaints about every little side effect like all they did was trade in one bad experience (depression), for an equally bad experience (side effects), I draw the line. That's totally untrue, and it discourages people from taking needed medication.

Did I love the farting situation? Not really. I didn't enjoy the drowsiness that comes with anti-depressants, or the fact that I seemed incapable of catching a second wind either. I prided myself on my ability to push past the point of exhaustion; medicine took that away from me. Boo-fucking-hoo, right? Now I'm not saying it's not difficult, because letting go of who we used to be is incredibly difficult. Change is hard, and it's a sacrifice worth recognizing. It's okay to struggle on the path to recovery. It's ok to be frustrated, angry, confused, lost, scared. I was. I was terrified, but it's not ok to throw a full on, woe is me, the sky is falling, pity party.

What really drives me up the wall though is people who call this medicine poison. I hear it most frequently from parents who say they don't want their child to be "poisoned" by "drugs," yet in the next breath explain to me how they allow their 24-year-old kid living in the basement to rip a bong whenever he needs to take the edge off because it's "healthier." It's not. Marijuana has a lot of medical properties worth exploring but ripping a bong to escape the existential burden of living is not one of them. What part of getting high every time you experience pain is healthy? Would anyone seriously claim it was ok if I drank any time I fell into despair? No. That's called alcoholism, and it's conclusively proven to be unhealthy. Smoking a joint is simply a temporary escape and allowing that behavior to continue reinforces the idea that it's ok to escape when inflicted with pain. Well, suicide is the final escape. It's the option chosen by people who believe they have no other options, which I unfortunately know from firsthand experience.

I'm not trying to be cruel or mean, but sometimes to truly help someone, you've got to take the kid-gloves off and go Old Testament on them. I'm not a parent, so I won't pretend to know what I would do in that situation, but I'll offer this; one of the reasons my parents helped me so effectively through depression was because there was no doubt in my mind they'd open a can of whoop-ass on me if I deserved it. If I threw away all my responsibilities and simply gave up. If I consistently treated others like garbage hiding behind depression as an excuse for my behavior. No one offered me more compassion than they did, but they would've brought the hammer down without hesitation if needed. That hammer put up boundaries. Those boundaries oriented me towards recovery. The idea of recovery motivated me to try the meds and taking them taught me they're not poison; they're lifesaving.

You can have reservations about the medicine, that's totally fair (I did). You can be hesitant towards them, skeptical of them, concerned for the effects they may have on you or someone you care about. That's all totally reasonable. Psychiatric drugs aren't as simple as Advil. These meds are supposed to change our thoughts, and we very closely identify our thoughts with who we are as individuals. What if we lose ourselves? What if the medicine drives us to insanity or worse? There's so many nutjobs out there these days, and the idea has been floated more than once that SSRI's, most modern anti-depressants, have some culpability in influencing people to commit horrific atrocities like mass shootings. I didn't want that to happen to me, and I often considered taking myself out to ensure it didn't.

That's why reaching out, building a network of people, is so critical to recovery. I told my Mom I was scared to death of taking anti-depressants. I didn't get into all the reasons why, just that I was afraid I'd lose myself, and she reached out to someone we both knew to talk with me about my fears. I was shocked to learn this person, who we'll call Elizabeth, suffered from depression earlier in her life and also needed anti-depressants along her path of recovery. The entire time I knew Elizabeth, she always seemed happy, full of life, and took pleasure in small joys. I never would have guessed she struggled with depression, just as no one would've guessed that about me.

She called me around the beginning of October. I had been taking the medicine for a few weeks and started feeling its positive effects, but I was so bent out of shape about losing myself part of me wanted to quit the meds all together.

"Hey Lucas, how are you?" she asked.

"I'm ok," I answered kicking at a pile of colored leaves. I didn't want anyone to overhear my conversation so I walked to a remote park so far away from campus it might as well have been in Narnia.

"And school's going well and all?"

"Yupp. Yeah it is. I'm passing my classes, though they're a bit easier than usual this semester."

"Well that's good. You deserve a little bit of a break."

"Yeah…" I replied, my stomach twisting itself into knots. We spent some time talking about the brutality of depression. We both lost the ability to eat and dropped a lot of weight. We couldn't sleep. We had nightmares. We pushed ourselves even after it became clear something was seriously wrong. The drivers behind our depression were vastly different, but the depression itself sounded mostly the same.

"I hear you're a little worried about taking the medicine," Elizabeth said when we got to the meat of the conversation.

"Yeah, I am."

"What has you worried about it?"

"I don't know. It's not like Advil, you know?" I said plopping into a swing to rock back and forth in an effort to calm my fraying nerves. "This medicine, it's for my mind. What if I lose myself? Or become a zombie? Or something worse?"

"I understand. It's scary. It really is, and I was a little nervous myself, but Lucas, it helped me within a couple weeks."

"Really?"

"Yes. Not a lot better, but after feeling worse and worse every day for what seemed like forever, it gave me hope when things started improving." I stopped swinging as the cold panic enveloped my body and mind once again. I was tired of it, so damn tired of it.

"Lucas, you there?"

"What if that doesn't happen for me? What if something bad happens?"

"What are you afraid will happen?" I didn't want to say what I was really afraid of. Tears filled my eyes, but I held them back (enough with the crying already, geez). My body trembled with fear, and I felt like I'd vomit and pass out.

"What if I hurt people?"

"Hurt people? How would you hurt people?"

176

"You've seen the news. These people, these animals that go shoot up a bunch of people. They're depressed and anxious and they say it's the meds that messed up their heads and made them do it. What if it messes up my head? What if it does that to me? I don't want to hurt anyone!" I said nearly hysterical.

"Lucas, no, no – that's not – listen to me very carefully. Those people – they have evil in their hearts. Ok? They're evil people. The medicine didn't make them do anything. They made a choice. There's no evil in you, Lucas. There's no evil in your heart."

I was surprised to hear Elizabeth say that; she's not a particularly religious person. Maybe that made it mean more. Regardless, what she said brought me peace. She reminded me we always have a choice. The medicine couldn't *make* me do anything. It couldn't take away my ability to choose, and that's what truly defines us, not our thoughts. Our thoughts are unruly; they can't be perfectly controlled. I couldn't stop the images of suicide that rolled through my mind no matter how much I wanted to, but those thoughts didn't define me. The choices I made to take medicine, to go to talk therapy, to fight for healing – that's what defined me.

Recovery's hard, but it is possible. Choose to travel the path of recovery, and I promise you won't be telling your story with a sigh somewhere ages and ages hence. And if you need to take medicine, you have a choice about that too; you can be bitter and resentful that you have to deal with unwanted side effects, or you can be thankful for the help medicine provides and laugh your ass off that it makes you fart when you drink milk because honestly that's hilarious.

The "Unbreakable" Story

After my conversation with Elizabeth, I put the worst of my fears aside and allowed the medicine to do its thing. It didn't cure me of depression, but it lifted the illness enough that I could work on what John taught me in therapy. At the top of his list was me relearning "what it means to be Lucas." I guess it wasn't lost on him that I was kind of adrift. I didn't know who I was after I broke. I was untethered, like Ant Man floating through the nothingness of the quantum realm detached from time and space. I needed something sturdy to lift me from that nothingness; therapy showed me how to build that something sturdy, but it took time. That was ok with John. "We're not in a rush," he'd tell me. "We didn't get here overnight. We won't get out of here overnight."

So, I relaxed. I stopped hurtling a thousand miles an hour and gave myself permission to chill. I didn't need to study till it hurt for it to be enough. I didn't need to apply to jobs until my eyes dried out from staring at a computer screen. I didn't need to solve the problems of the world for my life to have value. I let that all go and started over in defining what it meant to be Lucas. My Mom always said, "Before you can help others, you need to help yourself." I didn't necessarily believe I was supposed to help others, but I think deep down we all have a desire to make the world a better place in whatever way we can. My Mom was simply trying to tell me we can't do that if we're broken ourselves; to make the world better, I had to make myself better and believe that I deserved it. So that's what I worked on doing.

For most of September, I lived by the one-hour rule. I'd study in blips, workout in short spurts, and took the Klonopin as needed after my birthday. When I really had a bad day, I'd let schoolwork slide and go for a walk. Happy Valley's a wonderful place for a walk in the fall whether I trekked through frat row and the quaint neighborhoods behind my apartment or moseyed along campus with a herd of students. During these trips, I'd often call one of my parents just to talk. It helped me to not feel alone, and as I've said before, defeating isolation is key to defeating depression. I give them a lot of credit; they always answered and talked with me as long as I needed regardless of what they were doing. It helped a lot, and I needed that because September was the toughest month of my life. It dragged on *forever* like the credits of a movie when you're waiting for the after-credit scene. But it was a good month, and it gave me hope.

The Zoloft began kicking in during the later weeks lightening the load of depression. Most mornings I still woke up feeling like shit, but I stopped wishing I died in my sleep, so that was an improvement. Eating came easier too. I packed on about five pounds that month, and my ribs no longer protruded like I was a starving child. My face looked livelier, and I saw a hint of my former self in my eyes. The nightmares all but disappeared, and I didn't wake up half a dozen times over the course of a night anymore. John constantly said he wanted to tighten up my sleep, and as my condition improved with a regulated sleep schedule, I saw why.

As for my classes, it truly was the easiest semester I had since freshman year. I passed the first round of exams with B's across the board, though brain fog was so severe during one exam I forgot how to write my name in cursive, and on another I almost crapped my pants because of the meds so not exactly easy breezy. Doing well helped me because it was one less thing to worry about. People always say you should pay attention to your finances so when life's storms inevitably arrive, that's one less thing to worry about, and I think earning decent grades was the college equivalent of that age-old wisdom.

To top it all off, I was invited to more job interviews than I could attend. Even Albemarle offered me an interview after their representative said my GPA wasn't high enough. I couldn't believe it! After years and years of a steady, nearly 100% rejection rate, I took one step closer to the Holy Grail of college education; a job offer (I guess that internship in New Mexico wasn't for nothing). And I loved interviewing! It put me in a different state of mind, like an athlete in the zone or an actor prepping for a role, except I wasn't pretending to be someone else; I was just being me without the depression. During these interviews, I became a talkative, inquisitive, easy-going version of myself, and I liked that.

Then it was October. The leaves changed, the air was brisk, and comfy hoodies were taken out of the closet. I was excited about it, and that mattered. The me before depression used to always be excited when the seasons changed. Fall was a break from the heat. You'd start school and see your friends every day. Nature looked like something out of a painting. Everyone was obsessed with pumpkins and hayrides for a month. Then it got colder and there was Thanksgiving and Christmas and the first snowfall to look forward too. And just as everyone got tired of the cold, spring appeared thawing out the world and waking us from hibernation. Birds chirped. Bunnies hopped. Squirrels scurried about. Flowers bloomed, trees sprouted green, and everything burst with a sense of new life. As the days grew warmer and we longed to be outdoors, summer arrived, and we got our wish as rigidly scheduled days gave way to the ease of summer lounging. Then the cycle repeated. It always brought me joy until depression. Depression made me feel like I was stuck in a hamster wheel going nowhere. The changing seasons weren't exciting anymore; they were part of the pointless grind of life.

They filled me with dread and despair and the monotony of time, but in the October of my recovery, I felt a small spark of joy and knew I was getting better.

Then I talked with Elizabeth about the meds, and another fear of mine went out the window. I was no longer afraid I'd turn into a nutjob, and the peace of mind that brought me went a long way in reducing my anxiety. As I headed into November, about eight weeks into taking the Zoloft, I noticed the intrusive thoughts pretty much stopped. Graphic images of my suicide no longer tormented me. More days passed than not where I *didn't* think about taking my life, and I only suffered about one or two panic attacks a week, down from a dozen or more before I started the meds. I also stopped following the one-hour rule; I didn't need it anymore. I could handle a full day at a time. It's hard to describe how incredible of a turnaround that was, but I'll give it a shot.

Imagine you're drowning in the middle of the ocean. The choppy sea crashes over your head, and strong currents drag you underwater. You thrash about like a wild animal to get to the surface, only to be greeted by a wall of rain as you take a breath. The water blinds you. It fills your nostrils, your mouth, and then your lungs. Just as you're about to go under for good, a hand reaches out and pulls you aboard a sturdy ship. You're dazed and confused and as you give in to the blackness of unconsciousness, you're vaguely aware of someone telling you it's going to be alright. When you come to, you're dressed, dry, and sitting in a bed with a blanket over your shoulders. You venture out to the deck. The storm clouds are breaking up; they're no longer dark and menacing, but light gray with hints of white around the edges. The sun pushes its way through the cracks, warming you and lighting up the calm sea which peacefully rocks the boat with gentle, rolling waves.

"Told ya, you'd be ok," says an old man approaching you with two steaming mugs of tea. His face is weathered with kind wrinkles like that of a happy grandpa. He's dressed in overalls, a checkerboard flannel, and a woolen cap.

"The storm took me by surprise," you say, accepting the mug he offers you.

"It always does."

"Will it come back?"

"Time will tell," he answers looking out across the ocean.

"Is it up to me?"

"Sometimes."

"Is there anything I can do to prevent it from happening again?"

"Learn to swim," he says with a smile. When you don't return one, he continues, "Rest. Drink your tea. Don't worry about a storm that may or may not come." You try, but you can't. The memory of you nearly drowning is too fresh. You never saw the first storm coming, and it almost killed you. Would you see the next storm? Or would it destroy you just as thoroughly? Sure, you were on a boat now, but what if the storm was bad enough that it tossed you overboard? Or what if you made it back to land only to watch a loved one be swept away by *their* storm? Would you have the strength to help them, to save them? And if you didn't, would you try anyway only for the both of you to drown? Was it worth being rescued, or should you have just drowned in the first storm? Would that have been better for you, for everyone?

A rumble of thunder growls in the distance as the clouds turn a darker shade of gray. The sun disappears. The sea churns, tossing the boat about like a toy. You look at the old man with fear in your eyes. He seems unbothered sipping his tea.

"There is always a storm on the horizon. Learn to enjoy the peace of today, or you will forever sail through rough waters."

Learn to enjoy the peace of today. That was my next goal, but I was terrible at it. The brief joy I experienced from my initial recovery began giving way to fear depression would return with a vengeance. It destroyed me the first time, very nearly killing me. I didn't believe I had the strength to weather a second storm. I was powerless to stop the first one. If a second hit...

"You can't worry about that," John said, barely hiding his exasperation. This was the fifth or sixth time we talked about depression coming back, but I made no progress dealing with it. "Are you worried about Martians attacking us tomorrow?"

I rolled my eyes. "No."

"You get why I'm saying that though, right?"

"Yeah, yeah. We don't know if Martians exist. If we don't know, why worry what they might do tomorrow. Yadda, yadda, yadda."

"I'm serious."

"So am I."

"The possibility of depression coming back – it's the same thing as Martians attacking."

"If it was that simple, don't you think I'd stop worrying by now?"

"It is that simple if you'd let it be you idiot."

"No, it isn't! Depression broke me. It broke me..." I looked away humiliated.

"Did it?"

"I wanted a bus to run me over. 'What would you call that?' That's what you said to me."

"Yeah, yet here you are Superman."

"I don't feel like Superman. I feel fragile... weak."

"Well, was Superman who he was because he was strong, or because he did what was right?" I looked up at John as he continued, "When shit hit the fan, and damn did it hit for you my friend, you never lost your sense of what was right."

"So?"

"So! Dude, everyone goes to the Darkside for a little, but you didn't."

"So I didn't turn into more of an asshole than I already am. How does that matter at all?"

"Man, you really are a fucking moron." John and I both cracked up. I laughed so hard it took me about a minute before I finally said, "Yeah, I guess so because I don't see what you're getting at."

"You think depression broke you, but it didn't. Maybe it broke who you thought you were, but it didn't touch the best part of you because somewhere under all that jackass is a heart, and you have a rare one. That's the best part of you. That's what's good about being Lucas, what's always been good about being Lucas. Depression can never, and will never, take that from you. Your heart conquers depression, every time."

John was right; depression couldn't reach the best part of me. It can't reach the best part of you either. There is something in each of us that is unbreakable, that cannot be destroyed by the storms of this world. I already believed that; I've always believed that because of Gabriel. The doctors had no hope for him, and I don't blame them because they're people of science and the science said there was no hope for Gabriel. I believe very much in science too, but it often discounts the most important part of being human; our spirit. Gabriel defied science. He defied logic. He defied what was supposedly possible through the strength of his spirit. He taught me there is a piece of us that's unbreakable if we choose to have faith in our spirit.

I kept that faith the morning I called my Dad instead of taking my life, because in my heart, who I am, and who I've always been, is the kid who promised his father he'd be a builder. That part of me was unbreakable. It didn't dispel the fear that depression would come back, but it gave me the courage to let go and enjoy the peace of today. Find the unbreakable piece of yourself, your true self, and with it you will find the courage to enjoy the peace of today too.

The "Redemption and Other Side" Story

After John pointed out I was never truly broken, I managed to get my fear of depression returning under control. It didn't haunt me anymore. I learned to enjoy the peace of today, but that was far from my final lesson. Humans aren't stationary creatures. We're much happier when we have a goal to strive towards; without one, we wither like rotten fruit. For much of the semester, that goal was recovery. As I realized that goal, I needed something else to strive towards, something more. I needed a vision for the future, a vision for my life without depression. But I didn't believe I'd ever be free of it. I didn't believe there was another side to depression. Until I talked to Diane.

We spoke on the phone in late November. It was evening, but the days were so short then it seemed like night. The air was cold and crisp and pleasant against my face. I strolled along the sidewalks leading to Old Main, my favorite spot on Penn State's campus. Graduation was less than a month away, and I felt good, but there was still an emptiness in me I didn't know how to fill. Something was missing. That something was belief in life after depression.

Once again, reaching out proved to be a literal lifeline. I had known Diane for a few years and always found her to be happy and rosy with just a hint of sass like a Southern Mrs. Claus. I was dumbfounded to learn she struggled with depression for years. When she heard about what I was going through, she immediately offered to talk with me and help in any way she could.

"Hey honey, how ya doing?" Diane asked as soon as I answered the phone. "I'm so sorry for what you're going through sweetie. It just breaks my heart. It really does." Right away, I knew Diane understood; I could hear it in her voice.

"Thank you. I'm doing much better than I was, but sometimes... I don't know. It's hard."

"Oh, it is sweetie. It's one of the hardest things I've ever gone through. If you want to, and only if you want to, why don't you tell me everything?" And I did. I told Diane how for years I felt myself slipping away and just did my best to power through it. She told me she did the same. I told her how I felt guilty for struggling because of my perfect life. She said she felt guilty too. I told her I lost the ability to eat, and how I gagged trying to put down a bagel. She said, "Honey, I understand," and told me about a time she forced down a bowl of soup at a restaurant only to run outside and throw it up in the bushes.

"I ended up in the emergency room. I was crying and said to the doctor, 'I don't care what you have to do – if you've gotta cut my arms and legs off with no anesthesia – please just make this stop.' Did you feel something like that honey?"

"Yea. I told the doctor if I got hit by a bus, the last thing I'd feel is relief."

"Oh, I am so sorry. There just aren't words."

"I'm sorry you had to go through it too." I let out a long breath watching the fog collect in the frigid air before wisping away into the night.

"Do you pray about it, honey?"

"I do."

"So do I. It doesn't magically go away, but it helps."

"Yea, it does."

"Though you know what really helps sometimes? A big ol' margarita." We both laughed at that.

"I couldn't agree more," I replied. We spoke for a while about depression and anxiety, and I enjoyed our conversation. It was nice to know I wasn't alone in my experience; that I wasn't crazy, or narcissistic, or ungrateful. Other people from all walks of life struggled with the same guilt, confusion, dread, and despair, yet each found a way out of their darkness.

"Is there anything else I can do for you sweetie?" Diane asked as we neared the end of our conversation.

I hesitated for a moment, thinking of how to put into words what I felt. "Does it ever go away?"

"Yes. Yes, it does. You have to take care of yourself, but yes, it goes away."

"I don't see it," I said, my voice catching from the emotion.

"Oh honey! Honey, no. There's another side to it all. I know how hard it is in the throes of it. I couldn't see it either. But if you keep looking, you'll find the other side."

"How did you find it?"

"By holding on. Sometimes that's the best we can do."

"And you're happy now?"

"I am. So happy. So, so happy to be alive."

I believed her. Diane pleaded with me so passionately that I could feel how she ached to show me the truth of her words. It's the same passion I felt when I thought of Madison, and how I wished I could bring her back, so together, we could find a way to live. But I can't bring her back; I can't bring anyone back. I can only plead with you as Diane pleaded with me, beg you to believe there's another side to your pain because there is. I couldn't see it for myself, but I didn't have to. Diane saw it for me, and I trusted her. That gave me hope. I didn't need to see the vision of my future that very minute because I believed that one day, I could find it. That was enough.

As my final semester at Penn State wound down, I tried to simply enjoy myself. I didn't worry about grades anymore because I scored well enough on the second round of exams to ensure I passed everything. I didn't worry about a job either. After dozens of interviews, I accepted an offer from a company called Thermo Systems in New Jersey that works in industrial controls and automation. Getting a job and graduating never would've fixed me – I know that now – but damn did it feel good and that counted for something!

Then, in the blink of an eye, I stood on the floor of the BJC waiting to graduate like the victor of a righteous war breathing a sigh of relief that the worst of the horror had ended. Was I totally free of depression? Not by a long shot. I only treated the illness for about four months at this point, and it took me closer to a year to truly stand up straight again, but all the same, the worst had passed. It's like when you have the flu and there's that one awful day where you're just dead. You can't get out of bed. You can't eat. You can't even stay awake long enough to watch an episode of something on Netflix. That day sucks. Then there's the day after when you wake up with some life. You're still sick with a headache and stuffy nose and a cough, but compared to the day before, you're ready to rock 'n' roll. Keep taking care of yourself, and you'll be better in no time. That's where I was with my recovery at graduation, and it felt good.

I looked up into the stands to where my parents sat. I couldn't make out their faces without my glasses, but I knew it was them from the way my Mom waved using her whole body like she was part of a cheerleading routine. I smiled and waved back. She was excited, and why not be? Only a few months ago, John told my parents to be ready for me to come home from school. He thought I'd have to take the semester off with how badly damaged I was from my invisible illness. Others, with experience, told my parents to prepare for that scenario as well.

But to everyone's surprise, including my own, I clawed my way through the semester. Call it pride's parting gift; I was simply too embarrassed to fail (even though taking time off to heal is absolutely not failing – that's just how I saw it at the time).

Graduation was an abrupt yet satisfying end to the wild ride that was my college career. As the commencement speakers gave their farewell addresses, I reflected on all that I had gone through to get to that moment. Only a few months beforehand, I thought I was dead as I watched Joe graduate. Since then, I spent almost four months in New Mexico for an internship, crashed from depression, sought help, clawed my way out of Hell an inch at a time, passed my classes, secured a job, and reinvented myself entirely. Now I was ready to put a bow on the whole thing.

Row by row students stood up to waltz across the stage and receive their diploma, each with a smile on their face. I wondered what their diploma meant to them because I think it's always more than just a degree. What dreams had they fulfilled? What battles had they won? What memories flittered through their minds as they crossed the threshold?

Two rows in front of me stood up, and I continued reflecting on my time in college, the images flickering through my head like clips from a movie.

Joe and I arriving at Snyder Hall. Watching a play with Erica for our theater class. The student section breaking out in a spontaneous snowball fight. Opening fortune cookies with my friends in Pollock commons. Cramming a dozen people in a closet-sized dorm room and blasting *Send Me on My Way* while playing Nintendo.

The row in front of me was on their feet.

Nightmares haunting me as I declared my major. Drunkenly climbing through the second-story kitchen window of a frat that wouldn't let us in. Erica and I getting together in secret.

Bombing my first Chem E quiz. Sipping peppermint schnapps and playing SSX Tricky with Orto before a Wiz Khalifa concert. Tanking finals and struggling with the guilt that came with that.

My row stood up.

Moving into an apartment. Waking up in a closet on my 21st. Rejections piling up in my inbox. Playing foosball at the Gaff. Celebrating when the total was revealed at THON. Failing more exams. Telling Erica I didn't know what was wrong with me. Fighting the panic that plagued me. Running a marathon. Flying to New Mexico thinking I'd never make it home. Shooting a gun. Seeing my ribs poke out of my sides. Baring my soul to a stranger who seemed a bit quacky and wore crazy-colored shoes. Sitting on a bench by Old Main listening to the bells chime, filled with peace.

"Lucas. Anthony. Wolfe."

A pure, ear-to-ear grin washed over my face, and I strolled across the stage on the balls of my feet. Then they handed me my diploma, and for a second, everything simply stopped. It was more than just a piece of paper claiming I passed some classes in chemical engineering; it was a physical manifestation of all I had been through, of all the decisions I made, to choose life. No one made those decisions for me; only I could choose life for myself. I chose to get help. I chose to not become bitter. I chose to let go of my pride, to let go of myself, as painful as that was, to become someone better. All of this I did on the faith that it was right. When I received my diploma, that faith was confirmed, and I'll forever have that piece of paper to remind me of my commitment to life.

"You did it! You freaking did it," my Dad said as I found my family in the concourse. "I'm proud of you. I'm very proud of you."

"Thanks, Dad. I'm proud of me too."

"Me too," my Mom said. "Very proud." The tip of her nose was cherry red, a sign she was struggling not to cry.

"Don't go bawling on me Rudolph," I teased giving her a hug. That only made her cry harder.

"Congrats dude!" Joe said. "How's it feel?"

"Awesome. Like redemption." And it did feel like redemption, though it came with a twinge of fear and the question of "what's next?" because it seemed as if my whole life led to this point and now the path was wide open. Which way to go? That was a problem for another day. As Winston Churchill said, "Success is not final. Failure is not fatal. It is the courage to continue that counts." I failed a lot, and it didn't kill me. Now, I enjoyed success, but life didn't end with victory. Fortunately, John taught me how to find the courage to enjoy the peace of today, so that's what I did.

We left the Bryce Jordan Center, and my parents asked me what I wanted to do. It was a freezing December day, the kind of cold that cuts to the bone, but I told them I wanted to walk around campus anyway. Soak it all in one last time. They were a tough four and a half years, the toughest of my life, but also the best. I loved them! I loved college. I loved who I became. I don't remember the pain when I think of my time at Happy Valley. What I remember most is the day before Joe, Erica, and most of my friends graduated. It was a beautiful day in early May. Sunny and warm in the way that breathes new life into your limbs. We all chilled at Beaver Hill – me, Joe, Sam, Erica, Luke, Orto, Sumit, Brendon, Brandon – beers cracked open and reminiscing about our college experience. All day depression and panic plagued me, neither condition helped by the evening exam for Chemical Reactors that hung over my head, but in that moment the depression was gone. It was just gone. There was no reason for it to be, but it was. I didn't feel isolated or disconnected or outside of myself. I was a part of everyone's joy, each one of us happy for the other. It's the kind of moment you can only have when you let go of yourself to genuinely share in the happiness of others.

Then I had to leave for my final, but the moment didn't leave me. The sun warmed my body as I meandered to my exam. I put headphones in to listen to some music and Vance Joy's *Wasted Time* played. I remember thinking *nothing's a waste of time.* The trees bloomed with rich, green leaves hanging against the backdrop of a deep-blue sky. I stopped to marvel at the colors. *Thank you, God. Thank you for this life. It's good, life is good.*

I remembered that moment as I walked through campus after graduation still wearing my cap and gown. *Life is good.* Snow flurries danced around me. The cold air stung my face, and I heard my family's teeth chattering behind me. The tips of my fingers were numb, but I was warm.

Part II – The Other Side

After:

All This Life Left to Live

You know the best thing about kids' movies? All the underhanded, adult humor thrown into them. It's hilarious. Like when Shrek and Donkey approach Lord Farquaad's towering castle and Shrek says, "Do you think maybe he's compensating for something?" It takes some balls to throw a small-wiener joke into a kid's movie, which is probably why they're entertaining for all ages. And if the jokes weren't enough, there's always the morals. Every kid movie has a moral because kids learn more from listening to stories than being talked at; we all do.

One of my favorite kids' movies is *Kung Fu Panda*. Who would ever guess a chubby panda named Po would become the dragon warrior, the most fearsome warrior in all of China? No one, but that's what happens. Through an accident (though the kung-fu master claims there are no accidents and I kind of agree) Po is selected as the dragon warrior, the only warrior worthy of reading the kung-fu secrets contained within the dragon scroll. These secrets are supposed to give him the ability to defeat an evil enemy named Tai Lung who is on his way to destroy the valley in which Po lives.

Po undergoes extensive training and overcomes many hurdles in his quest to become a kung-fu master, while facing rejection from the other kung-fu masters because he is goofy, undisciplined, and does not fit the archetype of a traditional warrior (this is where "you're perfect just the way you are," adheres to its original meaning). But Po perseveres. He wins over his critics, completes his training, and is deemed worthy of reading the dragon scroll. However, when Po opens the scroll, he's horrified to find it's blank. There are no kung-fu secrets. There is no special ingredient to becoming the dragon master.

Discouraged, Po reluctantly agrees to leave home with the other villagers rather than fight for the valley. As he leaves town, his dad tries to cheer him up by talking about the new noodle business they will open.

"The future of noodles is dice-cut vegetables..." he says, oblivious to Po's dejection at failing to live up to the status of dragon warrior. "Maybe this time, we'll have a kitchen you can actually stand up in. You like that?" When Po doesn't answer, his dad turns around to see him sitting against the cart and letting out a heavy sigh, clearly feeling like the most worthless panda in all of China. He tries to comfort Po by offering to share the secret ingredient of his secret ingredient soup. Po doesn't look like he gives half a shit about the secret ingredient until his dad says, "The secret ingredient is... nothing!"

"Huh?" Po responds with wide-eyed amazement.

"There is no secret ingredient!"

"It's just plain old noodle soup? You don't add some kind of special sauce or something?"

"Don't have to. To make something special, you just have to believe it's special."

A look of understanding passes over Po's face. He unrolls the dragon scroll and sees his face reflecting back like looking in a mirror. "There is no secret ingredient," he whispers to himself. Po didn't need kung-fu secrets to become the dragon warrior; all he had to do was believe in himself. The ability to beat Tia Lung was within Po all along.

It may be a kid's story, but the idea of believing in oneself goes a long way towards beating depression. The illness is a collapse of hope as much as it is a chemical imbalance. If we believe we're worthless, and we don't try to get out of that belief, we can't overcome depression. It's not as simple as flipping a switch, but if we had *zero* control over our mental health, talk therapy wouldn't be an effective treatment. Taking ownership of our mental health is not the same thing as blaming ourselves; I don't blame myself. I don't blame anyone. But owning depression, acknowledging that some of my behaviors and thought patterns contributed to it, allows me to change and find freedom from the illness.

And that's the same choice we have if we suffer from a physical condition like high blood pressure. Plenty of people might not know they are genetically predisposed to high blood pressure. Maybe they consume an average amount of salt, but because of their predisposition it's too much, and the result is unhealthy blood pressure. No big deal the doctor would say. He'd prescribe some medicine and tell them to cut more salt from their diet. They do, and their blood pressure returns to a healthy level. Depression's the same thing only instead of eating different foods, you train yourself to think different thoughts. Go back to your old eating habits, and high blood pressure returns. Go back to your old thought patterns, and depression returns. I say that like it's simple, but it took me a good four years and a lot of ups and downs to figure out. As my Dad sometimes says, "I hope you can learn from my dumbass mistakes." I mean that because I have a lot of joy and fulfillment in my life now, and I hope it doesn't take you as long to find that as it did me.

So, that's what I'll talk about in this final chapter; how to find fulfillment in all the life you have left to life. I'm not a sage or guru. I don't have a 12-step program, and I can't guarantee

196

you anything except that it's possible – it's possible to find joy on the other side of pain if you want to. I'm just as much of a mess as anybody else, but I did find my way out of some sort of Hell, and I want to use what I've learned to help you get out too.

Holding on and Avoiding Boogeymen

"You could just sit out here forever, couldn't you?" Dolan asked peeking his head out of the air-conditioned hotel room.

"Yeah, I think so," I replied. We stayed on the third floor of a smaller hotel, one with four or five floors that gave it a homier feel than those sprawling high rises usually seen on Florida beaches. I sat on a lawn chair of the open hallway, watching as the sun set over the ocean with a cold Miller Lite in my hand.

"How do you not die from the heat? I'd be sweating my ass off out here."

"Lucas loves the beach more than anyone I know," Seamus said joining the conversation. "He'll sit in the sun for hours and melt."

"Sounds terrible."

"To each his own, boys" I said raising my drink. Dolan popped back into the room to grab a few beers, then came outside with Alex and my cousin Matt. We all toasted our drinks, then sat in silence for a few minutes to watch the sun set. The clouds drifting along the horizon were painted brilliant shades of orange, yellow, and pink while the ones floating higher in the sky turned a rich indigo matching the sea below.

"Well, it may be hot as balls here, but this is pretty nice," Dolan said breaking the silence.

"Yeah, thanks for putting this together, Luke," Alex added.

"Don't thank me. Thank Joe. He's the one getting married."

"We should all get married one after the other. That way we can go on a bachelor party like this every year."

"I think I need to make some more money before that."

"Amen."

"But, c'mon, that'd be cool. Hanging on a beach with the boys once a year slugging beers."

"For sure." We fell back into silence as the bottom edge of the sun slipped neatly behind the horizon like a CD gliding into a CD player.

"Does it have to be a beach?" Alex asked.

"Can be whatever you want," Matt answered.

"I kind of like skiing. That'd be cool to switch it up, ya know."

"Yeah, and I wouldn't mind going to Europe," Dolan chimed.

"I can't believe how much work sends you over there for travel."

"It's pretty sweet."

"You guys are lucky. My old job never sent me anywhere," Seamus joked. "I'm glad I got a new one."

"How's that going by the way?"

"Good. I like it. Still, forty-three more years till retirement."

"You know it."

"Work's not so bad," I said. "I like my job."

"You wanna do it for the rest of your life?"

"Don't know," I answered truthfully. "Hard to know what you wanna do for the *rest* of your life."

"I just want to start working and make that moolah," Matt added. He recently graduated college and wouldn't start working till the fall.

"Yeah, buddy!" Dolan agreed.

"Money's great, but you'll need more than that," I said.

"Like what?"

"Something to do with it."

"Like this?"

"Like this."

Purpose is the ultimate antidote to the purposelessness of depression. It's the end goal for beating the illness, but certainly not the first step. The first step is reaching out. That breaks the isolation of depression and begins to build some sense of community. No one does it alone. I used to think needing help was a weakness. People may speculate I thought that way because of my pride or, since I'm a guy, because of toxic masculinity. I've never been a fan of flippant, one-dimensional explanations for complicated issues, and this is no exception. I viewed needing help as a weakness because I misunderstood the role of independence in community. Independence grants us freedom which makes it a desirable and healthy trait to pursue. We aren't afraid of other people because we aren't dependent on them, so if they abandon us, or everything goes to hell in a handbasket, we can stand on our own two feet. In the absence of that fear, we can build trust – real trust – and that is the cornerstone of community. I thought asking for help meant I was dependent like a child that never grows up, and that my weakness would contribute to the deterioration of the community. I didn't want that to happen. But independent people stumble all the time. We fall. We get lost in the dark. Some of us even revert back to child-like dependence for a time, and that's ok as long as we don't take advantage of those who help us. That's the point of community; knowing there are people who will catch us when we fall just as we'll catch them when they fall, and we all fall. It's not weakness to acknowledge that truth. Asking for help when we need it doesn't make us wrongfully, pathetically dependent; it makes us good members of the community.

The second step is to have faith in what you know, not what you feel. If you wait until your depression is severe enough to contemplate suicide, then you know your feelings are royally screwed up. You can't trust them. I didn't trust mine. When my depression was at its worst, I *felt* as if my entire family could die in a horrific accident, and I wouldn't bat an eye. I *knew* that wasn't true, but feelings are much more powerful than knowledge. Knowledge disconnected from feelings has about as much strength as a limp noodle. It's a David versus Goliath battle every day. The thing about that battle is David always wins as long as he keeps the faith. Keep faith in what you know, be skeptical of what you feel, and you'll find the strength to hold on.

And while you hold on, begin to reshape how you see yourself. Let go of the idea that you are a static being with immutable properties like a slab of concrete. People aren't like that. Instead, view yourself as a lump of clay which you have the power to mold into any shape you want. That's closer to the truth, and it's good to know because we all have to change to overcome depression. And we don't have to change because we are wrong, bad, or stupid, we simply need to find a better way. Cut yourself some slack; it's ok to struggle. Even if our lives are perfect, it's hard to find our way, and we should never feel bad about that. I did for a while until my Mom said, "Lucas, it's not an either or. How great your life is doesn't take away from how hard this moment is, and how hard this moment is doesn't take away from how great your life is. It's both."

In the same vein as cutting yourself some slack, guard yourself against blaming others, and for the love of God avoid blaming boogeymen. Do not blame corporations, the government, society, God, the world, technology, the 24-hour news cycle, or any other such unchangeable entity. That is the path to destruction. If you go down that road, bitter resentment for life itself will consume you, and hatred for humanity will corrode your soul. I know because I took a step towards resentment, and seeing where that path led, I turned back and went the other way.

I saw that if we blame someone or something we have no control over, we'll never heal. It might very well be someone else's fault. One or more of these boogeymen might have culpability in your pain, but if you wait for them to change so you can be put back together, it'll never happen. Own your depression, own your pain, and you'll begin to find your way out of it. People don't always want to do this. I've heard many stories and have seen with my own eyes people who wear their mental illness like a badge of honor. Worse than that, some appear to participate in a race to the bottom, a veritable contest on who soldiers through the worst hell. The following is an excerpt from an article I stumbled upon perfectly describing this scenario:

"The people there went on and on about their various mental health issues as if they were badges to be put on girl scout sashes. One after the other, they one-upped each other. 'You have depression and it sometimes affects your day? Well I have depression and I can't even do my homework!' 'Oh yeah, well I have to stay in bed for two weeks sometimes!' 'Well I tried to kill myself once!' These are not trivial things…"

I agree; this stuff isn't trivial. It's patently insane to wear an illness like a badge of honor. Notice I said 'illness' and not 'mental illness' because if someone wore high blood pressure as a badge of honor, we'd think they were a nutjob. If they walked around saying, "Yeah, I've got high blood pressure. It's giving me heart problems, but you know, that's just who I am, and I live with it the best I can," we'd be like, "Uh, you know there's stuff you can do to fix that, right?" (or at least to try to fix it). And I get why this happens. Talking about mental health used to be taboo. It was a real hush-hush, hope-it-doesn't-happen kind of thing. People were shamed for their struggles and derided as weak, pathetic, or crazy. Well-meaning people sought to correct that misconception by being unashamedly open about their mental health in an effort to reduce the stigma surrounding it. That's a great thing, and it's helped many people, but somewhere along the lines, not so well-meaning people hijacked mental illness and jammed it into a tier on the victim-privilege hierarchy (I'll talk about this a bit more in a later story). That is not a good thing because we do not like to let go of our identities, especially identities we are proud of. If we define ourselves by our mental illness, and we're proud of that, we won't heal.

The right way to view mental illness, I believe, is with sober acceptance. It's just a thing I deal with (again, the same as high blood pressure). Make a few changes, get it under control, and you mostly won't notice it anymore. Sure, you've got to continue to take care of yourself, but it won't forever consume your life the way it does when you initially start digging out of that hole.

As you heal, allow yourself to enjoy life. Live at a slower pace. Go for a walk. Read a book. Take a nap. Do something that quiets your mind and helps you enjoy the peace of today. Believe that there is a purpose to your pain, to your life, and to everyone's life. Do this without burdening yourself. You don't need to know the purpose, not right away. It's enough to have faith in the hope purpose offers. And if you hold on, if you keep looking, you'll find your purpose one day.

Finding Purpose at Chick-Fil-A

"I didn't ask for this."

"No, you were born with it, so don't cop out behind 'I didn't ask for this.'"

I thought about those lines from *Good Will Hunting* often as I went about my life post-graduation. What did they mean? Will was dealt a crap hand in the game of life, but he was also given an ace in the hole; his Einstein-level genius. Why did he run from that gift? When he said, "I didn't ask for this," what he really meant was, "It's my life, my gift, and I can do what I want with it including throw it away." Sean's simple response was, "Bullshit. Don't be a coward."

Harsh.

That response wouldn't fly in today's society. There's a fairly prevalent idea out there that, "It's my life. I can do what I want with it and to hell with everybody else." Once again, I think the root of that idea comes from a place of compassion, but at some point, it transformed into a philosophy of destruction. Part of what saved my life is that I didn't view it as simply *my* life; if I destroyed myself, I'd destroy others as well. My suicide wouldn't happen in a vacuum. So, if my life wasn't *just* mine, maybe the gifts I was given weren't just mine either.

This implies I have a responsibility to myself, and even more so to those who don't have what I have, to use the gifts I've been given. This point is made later in the film when Will is talking to his best friend Chuckie about the future, and Chuckie says he'll kill Will if he's still working construction in twenty years. Will understandably looks stricken, and Chuckie tries to explain, "Look, you've got something none of us have—"

"Oh, come on. Why is it always this?" Will says cutting him off. "I mean, I fuckin' owe it to myself to do this or that. What if I don't want to?"

"No. No, no, no fuck you. You don't owe it to yourself. You owe it to me. Because tomorrow I'm gonna wake up and I'll be fifty and I'll still be doing this shit and that's alright that's fine… But you're sitting on a winning lottery ticket and you're too much of a pussy to cash it in. And that's bullshit."

Again, harsh.

But tomorrow Gabriel's going to wake up and he'll be fifty. He'll still need someone to take his urine-soaked diapers off in the morning. He'll need someone to help him shower, to dress him, feed him, brush his teeth. He'll need someone to take him to chair yoga, to play tennis baseball with, and to take him to work. He'll need someone to turn on the TV so he can watch *Elmo*. He'll need someone to take him to the bathroom. He'll need someone to put him to bed. Tomorrow Gabriel's going to wake up and he'll be fifty, and he'll still need someone for every minute of his life. In light of that, who am I to waste what I've been given? No, I have a responsibility to Gabriel to do something with my life. We all have a responsibility to ourselves and others to honor what we've been given, no matter how much or how little, and that gives us purpose.

This all sounds a bit heavy, but it didn't weigh on me the way it would've pre-therapy. John helped me work through most of my guilt pointing out that I didn't actually waste anything, and even if I had, there's always the opportunity for redemption. He gave me permission to relax. To live at a slower pace. To enjoy life. He preached the same wisdom as my Mom about a broken person not being able to help others always stressing that there was plenty enough purpose in getting myself fixed to keep me occupied. So that's what I did.

After graduating, I moved back home because work was nearby. Initially, I was embarrassed to be home because I'm a Millennial, but I got over it quickly. It was nice to be with family. I liked getting up in the morning and saying hi to my parents. I enjoyed petting my dog before work. I didn't even mind the commute. It gave me time to listen to the radio, drink my coffee and wake up a bit.

Work was hard in the way all new things are, but I was used to not understanding much of anything from college, so it didn't bother me. I learned a lot of stuff I didn't know – how to set up a network, configure servers, design a control system – it was cool. And then work ended at 5pm. The rest of the day was mine to do what I wanted. Compared to college, I now had an eternity of free time.

Sometimes I'd talk with my parents when I got home. Or I'd hang out with Gabriel. Or I'd take Bolt for a walk. Other days I'd go to wing night at the local bar with my friends, shoot hoops with Dolan in the park, or roast marshmallows to make s'mores with Alex. Occasionally, I watched Netflix while working out, but if I was feeling lazy, I'd just watch Netflix. On the weekends, I either visited Erica in New York or we both visited Joe and Sam and our other friends in DC. Every now and again I'd just chill at home and catch up on sleep, maybe read a book or relax in the hammock in my backyard. Life was good, and I began to feel whole again.

I kept up that routine for about a year and a half, always getting a little bit better and a little bit stronger until one day I woke up feeling a little bit lost. Why was I doing any of this? Was I working so I could afford to relax, and relaxing so I could afford to work? That wasn't enough. Sooner or later I'd resent work, be bored of relaxing, and fall back into the pit of point-lessness. Did I work to build a future for myself? And if so, why? What was in that future? Why did it matter enough for me to strive towards it? Did I want to get married? Did I want to have kids and start a family? Why? Because that's what people do, that's what people have always done? Not enough. Why work? Why aim to better myself? Why live? What was any of it for? What's the purpose? What's *my* purpose?

I began to feel guilt again about the life I'd been given. Maybe I didn't waste it, but was I doing all I could with it, or did I settle because that's easier than striving towards a goal? How did I know if I honored the gifts, talents, and opportunities handed to me? Was I supposed to use the hand I'd been dealt in one, Hollywood-style event like Tony snapping to defeat Thanos? And if so, what became of my life after the snap? Did I still have purpose, or was my destiny fulfilled and everything after was meaningless?

I was long on questions but short on answers until one day when I visited Gabriel at the Chick-Fil-A where he works. He can't hear or talk or move around much on his own, so he can't take people's orders, prepare their food, clean up their trays, sweep the floor, or clean the bathrooms. That knocks out all the jobs there are at Chick-Fil-A, but the owners of a store near us got to know Gabriel and liked him so much they created a position for him. They made Gabriel a greeter. He opens the door for people.

Gabriel was shocked to see me and asked for a million hugs the way he always does when he's happy to see someone. Then I stood off to the side watching him work with the help of my Mom who made sure he stayed focused. As each person came into the restaurant, they'd see this twenty something year old kid, who's slightly chubby in a cute way, towering over a petite woman who is barely more than a hundred pounds soaking wet. He'd open the door for them with his left hand, his right usually tucked into his chest at an odd angle giving away his physical disability. Sometimes he'd put his foot against the door so he could sign 'hello' with his good hand, and other times he'd ball his bad hand into a fist for a fist bump. If he was in a really good mood, he might show you a trick he can do with his eyebrows where he raises them up and down at lightning speed. No matter what though, he always looked each person in the eye smiling at them with the cheesiest grin you ever saw.

Some who came through were regulars saying hi to Gabriel and giving him a hug. Others were new and asked my Mom about him. She'd say, "This is Gabriel, my peep," and explain that he was a Chick-Fil-A greeter. Everyone loved that idea even though they were perfectly capable of opening a door for themselves. It's different when Gabriel does it. He's got this way about him, this innocence and tenderness that cuts right through the pretenses we wear like shields. He reaches into a person's heart and gives them peace. He gives miserable people joy. He gives grieving people comfort. He gives hope to those in despair. Wherever Gabriel goes, he brings with him an undeniable sense that life is good. All he did was open a door, yet he changed people's lives.

No one asked what the purpose to life was as they walked into Chick-Fil-A; you could feel the meaning when Gabriel opened the door, and his heart, to those entering the restaurant. You could sense it in the loving bond between him and our Mom. Some things have inherent meaning in a way that falls short of words, but you know it when you see it and when you feel it.

It made me think of how Sarah treated me in New Mexico. She saved my life, but in her mind, I doubt she thinks she did anything. She was a good friend though, and that's rare to come by, especially these days. By doing that, she helped me find my way out of depression. By being a decent person, she shielded me daily from thoughts of suicide. You might be doing the same thing for someone right now and not even know it. We have no idea how deeply and eternally we impact people through the course of our everyday actions. Through something as simple as opening the door. Or helping someone who dropped their books on the way to class. Or inviting the kid with no friends to play football with the gang. You could save someone's life, and as the old Hebrew saying goes, "Whoever saves one life, saves the world entire."

Maybe I had this purpose thing all wrong. I thought there was one, grand, overarching reason for each of our lives; that there was one thing we were meant to do, and if we didn't fulfill that one thing, then we wouldn't fulfill our purpose. I thought of purpose like a train that comes through the station only once, and if you missed it, that was it, you missed out on your purpose forever. But that's not how it works. Purpose is a train that's *always* at the station. Always. It's simply waiting for us to acknowledge it and get on.

I found purpose from watching Gabriel at Chick-Fil-A. He showed me that everything matters; everything has purpose. The tough part of accepting this idea is if everything matters, then *everything* matters. That's a difficult burden to bear with a healthy mindset, and even more difficult if depression and anxiety addle your thoughts so you see everything in terms of life and death. Fail a test – dead. Get rejected from prom – dead. Lose a job – dead. That's no good. So I had to learn to see things in proportion. Everything matters, but not everything is life and death. When I found the balance, I found peace.

I'm not haunted by the purpose behind life anymore. I've found what I think it is – to build joy. It is through joy that burdens which cause us to grow weary are whisked away like fallen leaves taken by the wind. And joy is not the same thing as happiness. Happiness is the feeling we get when we open a present Christmas morning to find that it barks. Joy is what we experience after months of waking up every hour of the night to take the puppy out. After cleaning up countless accidents throughout the house, washing puke off our blankets, and playing with the endless supply of energy five times a day even when we're dead tired because that's what's best for the puppy. Then, when we come home from school or work or wherever, and that dog's entire body is wagging because he's so happy to see the person who cares for him (or her), that is when we know joy.

Always aim for joy because it can be accomplished in small steps and large goals. Joy's an idea that can orient us our entire lives acting as a North star to guide us through our struggles and direct our decisions. I wrestled with guilt over how to earn what life handed me believing whatever I did was never enough. But Chuckie didn't demand Will win the Nobel prize in mathematics, he simply said Will owed it to others to do more than nothing. That's all I owe, that's all any of us owe. To do more than nothing. To strive to build a better world even through actions as simple as opening the door for someone. This is what I mean by the idea of joy, and no other idea has worked so effectively to rid me of depression or given me as much strength to bear pain.

Compassionate Destruction

Guardians of the Galaxy is one of the most popular Marvel movies because it features a cast of misfits who have no clear moral compass, yet risk their lives working together to save the galaxy from a nearly invincible foe, Ronan. There's no incentive for them to fight this fight. Each of the Guardians has been screwed over by the galaxy in various ways. The people they're trying to save arrested them earlier in the movie, and Ronan is more powerful than all of them put together. They could simply tuck tail and run. They don't need to risk their lives, and they argue about what to do when they stumble upon an Infinity Stone – an object of unrivaled power – that the enemy is looking for.

"Just give it to Ronan," says Rocket, a genetically engineered raccoon who was arguably the most screwed over of all the Guardians.

"So he can destroy the galaxy?" Quill, the scrappy leader of the misfits asks.

"What are you, some saint all of a sudden? What has the galaxy ever done for you? Why would you wanna save it?"

"Because I'm one of the idiots who lives in it!"

Interesting. Rocket makes a good point about the galaxy never having done a thing for any of them, but Quill counters with a better one; they all live in the galaxy. Its destruction is their destruction. This idea applies to society writ large. We are members of it whether we want to be or not. Some of us have been screwed over by society, and some of us haven't, but either way, we should seek its betterment. Its destruction is our destruction, so if we see something wrong, we don't get to just throw up our hands in nihilistic surrender pretending we have nothing to do with it. We have the same choice as the Guardians; tuck tail and run, or face it head on and at least try to prevent further destruction.

That's what I hope to do with my life, and this book is just one part of realizing that hope. Deaths of despair, classified as a death occurring from alcohol, drug overdoses, or suicide, are on the rise throughout society. In 2017, more than 151,000 Americans died from deaths of despair; that's the highest number ever recorded and more than twice as many as in 1999. Something is going on. Hopelessness pervades society in a way it hasn't before. If we don't fix the root cause of our collective despair, we'll never turn the tide against this epidemic. I want to turn back that tide of death. I don't want anyone going through what I went through, and I certainly don't want anyone dying from suicide, so I question everything in an attempt to find the cause of our despair. A lot has changed in the last twenty years; God is mocked more than He's revered, families are broken, tight-knit communities have all but disappeared, globalization has created economic angst, technological advancement has led to a decline in people skills and a rise in isolation – somewhere in these changes we planted the seeds of our hopelessness. We should talk about these topics as loaded as they are with the potential to offend. What is a little offense compared to life? We need to approach one another in good faith to see if we can't find a better way forward together.

That's what I aim to do here by examining the idea of privilege, another idea born of compassion corrupted unrecognizably into an instrument of destruction. This subject is fraught with political implications, so I hesitate to wade into such toxic waters, but I don't mean any of this politically. I want to solve the problem of hopelessness, and much of it, I believe, stems from the corrupted notion of privilege. All I can ask of you is to hear me out and accept that I say what I say in good faith.

Society is riddled with structural inequalities, one of the more obvious being the ZIP code you're born into. If you're born in a community with good schools, the data says your chances of achieving a financially stable life are far greater than those born in an area with bad schools. This is a cold fact. We know inequities such as these exist, and the concept of privilege sought to reconcile these structural disadvantages. That is a good aim, however, that is not the current realization of privilege. Instead of creating awareness and compassion as originally intended, it has given way to envy and hopelessness.

The twisted idea of privilege claims that if we are in an unprivileged class, we are fucked (notice that inherent to the notion of privilege are classes and categories a.k.a. division, so it is an idea that immediately opposes building a united community). Since privilege is defined by immutable aspects of our identity such as race, ethnicity, sexual orientation, and the like, it is unchangeable. We cannot overcome or break free of the disadvantages life unjustly burdened upon us. What's worse is we are told these burdens would not exist if not for the privileged, who are similarly unable to change their status, foisting them upon the unprivileged. We are told these groups are locked in a struggle for power as the privileged seek to oppress what rightfully belongs to the unprivileged. Oppression is an evil, therefore, those who seek to oppress others are evil, and evil cannot be reasoned with; it must be annihilated.

If you don't believe the reasoning I've just laid out, watch people who use the word privilege often. They spit it from their mouths like a venom, their faces and bodies contorted to display bitter hate and resentment. They are not interested in building bridges; they seek to destroy what they regard as evil. Somewhere along the lines, this corrupted idea snaked its way into my heart, corroding my sense of self-worth like an acid. The guilt weighed on me and grew like a debt accruing interest, but I could never pay it off because I could never redeem myself for the sin of being born privileged. Consumed by unworthiness and guilt, I spiraled into depression culminating in the contemplation of suicide. I guarantee I am not the only one.

What truly tipped the scales in my decision to reject the notion of privilege (I'm not saying advantages and disadvantages don't exist – they do – but I reject the corrosiveness of privilege in favor of an idea that incentivizes building a better world which I'll explain in a moment), was a post I saw on The Mighty, an online community dedicated to supporting those with various health issues, especially mental health. The post essentially read, "I'm so sick of healthy people not checking their privilege. They don't know the pain depression causes me, but I wish they did. If you're not going to help me, you can go die for all I care." The post had tons of likes and comments of those agreeing with how awful the privileged and healthy are, claiming the world would be better off with them dead.

What the hell is wrong with people? That was my knee jerk reaction, and I stand by it. First, let's take a look at the logic here; this person equates being healthy with being privileged and being privileged with being evil, therefore, a healthy person is an evil person. That's stupid. It's also false and doesn't lend itself to the possibility of recovery. If you see healthy people as evil you won't want to be one, so you'll stay mired in depression forever choked by the chains of your own hatred. Obviously, these thoughts don't occur in a direct, linear, and conscious fashion, but they are there, and they do drive people to wish atrocities against each other.

Which brings me to my second point against privilege; at its most extreme, the idea drives people to feel justified in wishing death and destruction on those they perceive as privileged oppressors. That's messed up. We all want to be understood because that helps break down walls of isolation, but depression is a uniquely challenging illness to comprehend absent personal experience. Not everyone will get it, and some may not even try to. Once, when I was speaking publicly about my depression a guy from the audience called me a pussy. That hurt. I struggle with being seen as weak in the way someone struggling with anorexia fears being seen as fat. Does that give me the right to wish depression on him simply so he loses the power to hurt me? What kind of world would it be if we all treated one another that way? I don't know, and I don't want to find out.

The way I saw it, I had a choice; wallow in justified anger over the ignorant comment or let it go in thankfulness that this person doesn't understand the horror of depression. Tough choice, but once again, I didn't want anger to destroy me. If I could bring myself to hate one, I could bring myself to hate all. Besides, I didn't know a thing about that guy. Maybe he'd been through his own Hell, and it ticked him off to listen to me talk about how I struggled with depression in my perfect life. Would reacting in anger lead him to try and see things from my point of view? Of course not. It's not his responsibility to "get it," it's mine to explain depression persuasively with the willingness to bear the scorn of those unwilling to act with compassion. Is that fair? No. But who cares? Now I can continue speaking about what I went through to inspire hope without fear of what a few negative Nellies might say. And if one of those Nellies does say something, I've positioned myself to be filled with gratitude instead of consumed by anger because I'm thankful they don't know the scourge of depression.

And there's the answer to the problem of privilege; gratitude. Always gratitude. Gratitude over anger. Gratitude over hate. Gratitude over guilt, especially over guilt. As for how to account for our unequal starting positions in life, I believe the answer lies in viewing each life as a blessing. I know that's simplistic, but each of us has different gifts, whether it's a mind capable of earning a degree in chemical engineering, or a heart capable of changing someone's day by opening a door for them. If we focus on what others have, we'll never find joy or peace in what we have. That doesn't mean we shouldn't work to build a more perfect union as Abraham Lincoln would say, only that if we focus on what we have in gratitude for it, joy will fill us instead of guilt or envy.

Think of this idea like a tower of cups where you're the top cup. When you choose gratitude over guilt or envy, you are filled and filled and filled until you are so full of joy you can't contain it anymore. It spills out of you to those closest, and as they see that you're full because you chose gratitude, they'll choose gratitude and be filled as well. As they are filled, their joy will pour out to others, and so on and so forth. But if we choose envy or guilt, not only will we not be filled, but we may empty those around us as if a twenty-pound dumbbell were thrown into the tower shattering it entirely.

This analogy helped me understand what my Dad meant all those years ago when he said, "People don't want to do the work to be a builder." Constructing a tower of cups and filling it (choosing gratitude despite many reasons to rightfully be angry at the world) takes time, effort, and patience. Tossing a dumbbell into the tower (choosing guilt or envy over gratitude) takes no effort, no time, no patience; only a willingness to destroy what others have because you don't personally have it.

I wanted to be angry about my experience with depression, and maybe I have a right to be, but I don't want to live that way. That's a decision to be made when you pull yourself out of the darkest depths though, not when you're at the bottom. Maybe you don't have to decide to be thankful today. Maybe you don't have to decide to be thankful tomorrow. Maybe all you need to decide right now is that one day you'd rather be thankful for the worst experience in your life than angry about it, because if you can be thankful for the worst that's happened to you, think of how much joy you'll have for the good.

Something Larger Than Myself

My Mom-Mom lay in a hospital bed dressed in a blue and white checkered gown. Her prognosis wasn't good, but the smile on her face showed how much she cared about that. The tubes hooked up to her the last time we saw each other were taken out. Her yellow-blonde hair wasn't matted down either; it had its characteristic small curls, like ribbons on a present. The incessant clicking and beeping of the droning machines fell silent, and the ambiance in the room was that of a pleasant Christmas morning.

"Do you remember the time when Pop-Pop, turkey that he is, got lost at the mall?" she asked me as we held hands.

"Yeah," I answered with a laugh. I remembered it well. My Pop-Pop had moderate dementia at the time and frequently became confused, yet insisted on traveling across the food court on his own to get a small coffee from Wendy's. We kept an eye on him the entire time and noticed when he stopped searching for our table indicating he was lost. He didn't look around in fear. He didn't ask for help. He didn't become agitated. He simply stood there smiling, contentment etched into the lines of his face as he sipped on his baby-sized coffee from Wendy's.

Those Christmas shopping trips to the mall with my grandparents were some of my favorite times as a kid, so it was no surprise my Mom-Mom wanted to talk about them. We also talked about bowling and card games, the Phillies and *The Price is Right*, college and eating McDonalds for dinner when her and Pop-Pop watched us.

Then the mood changed, and my Mom-Mom said, "It's time for me to go."

I gave her a hug. "Thank you, Mom-Mom. For everything."

The walls around us dissolved into swirling clouds like the eye of a hurricane. A rushing wind filled the room whisking my Mom-Mom away in her hospital bed. She waved as she went. The clouds closed in around me gradually fading to black, then I woke up. My Mom-Mom passed away that night, but no one needed to tell me; I knew because some part of me was with her when it happened.

If I told you I thought this was the Universe's way of letting me say goodbye to my grand-mom, most people would nod along in agreement, but if I said I thought it was God letting me say goodbye, a good percentage of people would call me a moron. They'd say it was simply a dream surrounding an emotional moment in my life. They're probably right about that, but does that mean it wasn't God? When we got the news Mom-Mom wasn't doing well, I prayed for the chance to say goodbye, went to sleep, had that "dream," and woke to learn she had passed.

Thirty, forty, fifty years ago almost nobody would ridicule me for believing God answered my prayer. Now? Not so much. God's been tossed out of society faster than Facebook took over Myspace. And I get it – I really do – because for so long God has been viewed not as an infinite being providing us with direction, but as an explanation for the inexplicable. He's become almost indistinguishable from the mythology that explained seasons, the creation of the world, human nature, and much more. But all of these myths have been dispelled by science, so what do we need God for? Isn't He just another story in a long line of stories meant to explain what we didn't understand in our primitive years? Ten thousand years ago, we couldn't possibly know about the Big Bang. Hell, five hundred years ago we still believed Earth was the center of the Universe. But science showed us otherwise; the church was wrong. Way wrong. So wrong, it labeled the heliocentric solar system a heresy, banned books promoting the theory, and put Galileo on trial essentially forcing him to recant the truth. Yikes. I wish that were the only incident between science and religion, but the two have a strained history with the church often being proved wrong. So, what reason is there to continue believing in God?

Whether you believe in Him or not, the idea of God and religion is inseparable from the collective human experience. Growing up in a Catholic household, I've questioned that experience nearly my entire life. It's part of my nature, I think. I've always been inquisitive wanting to know how things work and why. When I was young, I was obsessed with dinosaurs, fascinated by the gigantic creatures that roamed Earth for millions of years before going extinct. Somehow that topic led me to volcanoes and rocks, which led to tornadoes, hurricanes, weather, meteorology, the atmosphere, space, stars, galaxies, and eventually the universe. At some point, I questioned how this universe began, riveted by the seemingly unbridgeable gulf between science's explanation and religion's. Call me a nerd if you'd like, but I enjoy pulling on threads and seeing how far down the rabbit hole they go.

I thought of rejecting God for all the typical reasons that people do. If God exists, why is there so much evil in the world? Why is there so much suffering? Why is there hunger and starvation, war and violence, despair and death? Why is life so blatantly and wholly unfair? If He is all good, all loving, all powerful and the Creator of all things, then why create something that had the potential to go bad? Why make a Heaven and Hell and put us on Earth to blindly choose which one we want to go to forever? Why not create Heaven alone and place us there so we never have to suffer? And even assuming that there is a reasonable answer to all these questions, and assuming the Fall is real, why did we need redemption for our sins? Couldn't the all-powerful God simply wipe them away? Why did He have to send Himself to us in the form of His Son (a mystery of Christian faith I still don't understand) to be tortured and murdered as a sacrifice for our transgressions? The complexity of this idea, of God becoming man and allowing Himself to be destroyed by us for our own good, kept me from rejecting God outright. There are many rabbits to chase within this concept.

The idea of God becoming a man is not a uniquely Christian idea. However, God becoming a poor man, becoming the lowest among us, is uniquely Christian. Jesus was born in a manger among animals. That's incredible; Zeus would never subject himself to such humiliation. And throughout His life, Jesus went through all the worst of human experiences; loss, betrayal temptation, ridicule, torture, and death. Yet His message of love never wavered. That didn't answer any of my previous questions, but it did keep me from rejecting God as the dumbest of dumb ideas.

And I did think it was dumb. I can't tell you how many times I sat through mass feeling like the king of fools surrounded by a sea of foolish sheep. That includes my parents. Except neither of them are foolish sheep. My Dad is a mechanical engineer, someone who holds math, science, and logic in high esteem, thinks independently, and takes nothing at face value. And my Mom is probably the wisest person I'll ever know. So, how did these two intelligent, wise people believe in something as nonsensical as God? Especially when they had so many reasons, Gabriel chief among them, to not believe? Maybe because faith in God wasn't as nonsensical as it appeared to be. Maybe I just didn't get it. So, I prayed about it. Somewhere I read something that said, "If you struggle with faith in God, pray to Him." Seems like a bit of a catch-22, but I figured why not?

There's a story in the Gospel about a man who humbly approaches God asking for forgiveness. He barely enters the temple and does not lift his eyes to the altar but instead places his hand over his chest simply asking for mercy. The thing that strikes me about this story is the man doesn't come off as afraid, only aware of his own imperfection. I think I'm a lot like that guy except I don't know if I even made it into the temple when I prayed. A lot of times I didn't know what to say. I just sat there feeling helpless and stupid, hoping my unformed plea for guidance somehow floated to God's doorstep. And I guess it did because by the time I graduated high school, even though I felt lost, I believed I'd be led where I was supposed to go in the same way I allowed others to lead me out of depression when I couldn't see the way myself.

I held onto that faith because as I looked at the people in my life, I noticed commonalities between those who were happy, and those who were not. All the happy people believed in something larger than themselves; all the people who weren't, didn't. I'll give you an example. Many people have approached my parents over the years to tell them they should've put Gabriel in an institution saying things like, "It's your life. You only get one. Why should you deal with this?" Without exception, these people are miserable. And my parents, for all their suffering, are fulfilled. How is that possible? How is it possible that those who endure pain and suffering are more full of joy than those who run from it? Because at the end of enduring pain for something larger than ourselves is purpose, but at the end of pursing only our own selfish desire is nothing.

This idea wasn't articulated for me as clearly back then, but I understood it at a gut level. Observing the stark difference between those who were fulfilled, and those who were perpetually angry, I opted to follow in the footsteps of the fulfilled. Of course, that decision played right into the famous words of Karl Marx when he claimed, "Religion is the opiate of the masses." Did I believe simply to dull the pain of life without faith? It's a fair question, but the answer is no.

There's always been one aspect of God and religion that no one has been able to adequately explain to me if the world truly exists without a God; the miracles. The visions, the blessings, the answers to prayer like when I got to say goodbye to my Mom-Mom. The near-death experiences when people come back with stories of Heaven. Just in the last few years, two movies were made chronicling famous near-death experiences. The first was *Lessons from Heaven* about a young girl plagued with health issues who has a fall from a tree that should've killed her yet wakes up recovered from her incurable illness. The other was *Breakthrough* about a teenage boy who falls through the ice, sits at the bottom of a lake for 15-minutes, has no pulse for an hour, then walks out of the hospital two weeks later like nothing happened. Both young people recount images of Heaven and an afterlife. Are either of these stories proof positive of God's existence? No, not at all, but if it doesn't pique your interest, I'd encourage you to cultivate a better sense of curiosity.

Anyway, now you're caught up on my thoughts about God, how I struggled with my faith, and how I'm deeply fascinated by miracles. That's important for this next part because I've told you that things happened to me throughout my years in college to convince me I was on the right path. These events wouldn't have as much significance if you didn't know how much I've struggled with my faith.

It's no secret I struggled to declare a major and settle on a life direction for years. All that time I prayed to be pointed in the right direction, not to earn a lot of money or become successful (though I wouldn't mind those things), but simply to not waste my life. Despite feeling drawn to chemical engineering like metal to a magnet, I never really got an answer. Until Christmas break of my sophomore year right before I took my first Chem E class.

I seriously thought about switching out of the major last minute because part of me believed I enrolled only out of guilt. I knew I'd never make it through engineering if that were the only reason, so I wanted to change before I had to quit. But I took a second to pray about it, and a few minutes later had the urge to check my email – something I *never* did over break. I followed my gut though, checked my email, and had a message from my Mass Balances professor. He welcomed us to the major, told us his course was the easiest Chem E course we'd ever take, and explained a bit about how core curriculum courses work. None of it was very interesting except for the email sig-nature. Under the professor's name it read:

For I was hungry, and you gave me food.
For I was thirsty, and you gave me drink.
For I was naked, and you clothed me.

These lines are from my favorite Gospel passage because of their simplicity. Even those who are non-religious enjoy these lines because of their universal appeal, and it's one of the reasons I believe. It's a call to build a better world, and in a time when religion is a radioactive third rail, this is a message we can all get behind. What are the chances it was in this particular email, the first email I ever read on break? An email from my public college engineering professor, the type of person most likely to sneer at back-water hillbillies who believed in some-thing as childish and unenlightened as God? I'd say the chances were close to zero, yet there those Gospel words were pointing me in the direction of chemical engineering like a lighthouse guiding a ship to shore. I asked; God answered (though it took a few years). Imagine my surprise when I failed the class.

Talk about a slap in the face. But others went through much worse while retaining their faith to the point where my problem looked like a day at the beach in comparison. It didn't stay that way for long though. I didn't realize my battles in Chem E were proxies for the larger war with depression. Despair ate away at me bit by bit until I was a shell of my former self, a mirage that looked well but was hopelessly broken. When I failed Chemical Reactors in my senior year, that was it. That was depression's knockout punch, it's death knell, the song before the gallows. Even now, knowing it was the illness that broke me, I still feel shame that a failed exam represented the blow which shattered my last vestige of hope. But it did.

Except on the way back to my apartment, Cody, one of my good friends in Chem E, stopped me at the place where we split ways.

"Hey man, do you mind if I share something with you," he asked, seemingly uneasy as if he didn't know how to say what was on his mind.

"Sure, what's up?" I replied without interest.

"So, as you know, I try to pray a lot," he stammered. "And sometimes, I try to be still, and just listen to God. And, I just try to listen to what He's saying to me." Everything around us faded away into the background and I could only hear Cody. "Sometimes, I feel He puts something in my heart – I feel God puts something in my heart, and I have to act on it."

My heart raced and cold panic swirled within my gut ready to burst throughout me at a moment's notice. I wanted to run away. I was afraid, but I needed to know what he had to say.

"The other day when I was praying, I felt God put it in my heart to tell you... to tell you He loves you. God loves you. He wants you to know that."

"I... I... I don't know–" was all I managed to get out. The panic vanished and warmth spread through me like the sun melting frost off a budding flower. "Thank you. I needed that." Cody and I talked some more about God and life and if there was a plan to all of it, then I headed back to my apartment. As I walked across the sidewalk, I looked up to the sky thinking, *it's gonna get a lot worse before it gets better, isn't it? That's ok. It's ok, just please don't leave me.*

Maybe getting to say goodbye to my Mom-Mom was just a dream, and maybe those Gospel lines in my professor's email were a coincidence, but I'll never be convinced that Cody's message was anything other than a miracle. It didn't make any sense why God would pay attention to someone like me. I was a drinking, sex-fueled, casino-loving, egotistical ass. To the devout, I was barely more than a heathen. Yet in the moment I thought about throwing my life away, He sent someone to tell me I was loved.

I'd like to tell you it all makes sense to me now, but I still don't have answers to most of my questions and maybe I never will. Maybe none of us ever will. I'll tell you this though – I don't believe anything happens in vain. Not even suicide. Madison may have lost her battle with depression, but I'll always carry her in my heart, and that means something. It has to. Maybe that's small comfort to those who are suffering through tragic loss, but it's what little I can do to try and build something better.

As for chemical engineering being the path I was meant to walk, I think it granted me the perseverance I needed to fight through depression. Studying the subject taught me an array of new skills I used to overcome the illness; I'm not sure the person I was beforehand would've been able to do it. As for the depression itself? Hard to say. Diane told me she thinks she went through her depression to help me through mine. I'm on board with that. If the purpose of life is to build community, I can't think of a more lasting way to do that than to carry each other through Hell to a better life on the other side. Is it worth it? Yes, but that also depends on where you are on your journey. If you're at the bottom, you'll think there's no way I went through what you're going through because no one could ever possibly think that pain's worth it. Like I said, I was mad at first. It took me years to find my way to thankfulness, and for a while, I didn't want to be thankful for what I went through. I only moved toward gratitude when I discovered anger would throw me back into an even deeper pit of Hell.

Now, I'm thankful for my experience with depression. I feel so incredibly blessed to have the opportunity to reach out to others and show them they aren't alone. On top of that, I love who depression made me. I'm different than I was before. Pride no longer threatens to derail my life. Simpler experiences give me greater joy. I'm less stubborn, less selfish, more compassionate. I've still got innumerable imperfections, but I'm better than I was, and that's at least progress in the right direction. I only managed to get here because I believed in something larger than myself. For me, that something larger is God, but I understand not everyone will make the same choice and that's fine. I respect that but find something larger than yourself you can commit to, like building joy.

Having that something larger helped me let go of anger in favor of gratitude because I believed there was purpose to my pain. Purpose gives us hope, and hope gives us a vision for the future. This allows us to bear suffering, and to bear it with grace. So, if ever you find yourself in a dark and despairing place, please know that there is another side to your pain, and on that other side, is a rich, wonderful, beautiful, fulfilling life that you deserve.

All This Life Left to Live

I placed the wolf cufflinks on the dresser next to my phone so I wouldn't forget them in the morning. Joe got them for all his groomsmen as a gift for the wedding (not a bad gift considering our last name is Wolfe), then I climbed into bed where Erica was already half asleep. She seemed to sense me next to her throwing an arm over my chest and wrapping her feet around mine while muttering, "Toes." I laughed and saw a smile stretch across her lips even as she kept her eyes closed. The "toes" thing was a joke between us after our first Thanksgiving together.

Not long after I graduated in December 2015, her family found out we had been dating in secret for years. They kicked her out, as we knew they would, but that didn't make the pain any less intense. Erica handled the disownment of her family with grace (it was her tenderness in the face of such gross mistreatment that helped me to eventually let go of my own anger), though the first few months after the separation were difficult. She'd go through periods of sadness torn between the new life she was building and the loss of her family. The holidays were particularly hard, and that first Thanksgiving was no exception. We spent the Eve at my parent's house cleaning all day to get ready for the rest of the family to come over. That night we lay in bed exhausted, and I was nearly asleep when Erica whispered, "Lucas?"

"Yeah?"

"Our toes are touching."

"Yeah they are," I said laughing a bit, though I stopped when I felt a tear slide off her cheek onto my shoulder. "Are you crying? What's wrong?"

"I'm just so happy our toes are touching. I love you. You're my family. We're a family. I hope our toes touch every night forever because then I'd be happy forever." With that, she fell asleep, but I lay awake most of the night just thinking. How could she be so happy about our touching toes, especially after everything she'd been through? Her and I were family, but we still had a lot to figure out; the future was far from certain. But Erica didn't need all the answers right that minute. Sometimes it's enough to just enjoy the simple happiness of small moments. I wasn't even a year into recovery at this point, so it was good for me to learn not to take everything so seriously. I needed to understand that, because when you rebuild yourself, you won't get it right on the first try. I didn't.

I didn't get it on the second or the third or the fourth try either. Each attempt to build and subsequent collapse back into moderate depression taught me a new lesson about life and how to better myself. Each experience proved to me more and more that humans aren't just a bag of chemical reactions and electrical impulses; we have a will, and we can reinvent ourselves again and again and again. It took me a couple reinventions until I could truly see a future again, and that happened on the day of Joe and Sam's wedding.

That morning, while Sam and the bridesmaids started on their makeup, Joe and us guys went to the driving range to hit some golf balls. Even though it was the end of September, the heat was blistering, and we all got eaten alive by mosquitoes. It was still fun though, and Joe needed to do something to keep him occupied in the morning because he was more anxious to get married than he was to speak in front of a room full of people.

"Dude why am I nervous about this?" he asked later as we changed into our tuxes.

"Why wouldn't you be nervous?"

"I don't know. Sam's not."

"Oh, she's nervous she just doesn't know it yet."

"You think so?"

"Yeah dude. She's marrying you! Still not really sure why..." Joe dropped his hands to his sides looking at me with narrowed eyes and flattened lips in a classic Joe expression that said *Really?!*

"Has anyone drug tested her since you got down on one knee?" I asked.

"Ha-Ha." Joe took a step back from the mirror fiddling with his bowtie. He reached up tapping the top of his reddened ear muttering something about "stupid ears."

"It'll be fine Joe. Once you see your beautiful bride walking down the aisle, and she sees your goofy ass up there waiting for her, neither one of you will be nervous anymore." That got a genuine laugh out of him and he appeared to relax a little which was good because he and Sam deserved to enjoy their wedding day.

Everything went off without a hitch. Their nerves left as the ceremony got underway, and the two of them were all smiles. So was the crowd. As I stood next to Joe, I looked out to see all of our friends and family there to celebrate the new life he and Sam would create together. We were all a part of their old, separate lives, and now we got to be a part of their new, joined lives. What a gift. There was an entire world outside of this wedding, but in that moment, the entire world was just their wedding. And I was present. I lived my life; I didn't watch someone else live it anymore.

As the ceremony neared its end, I handed the rings to the pastor who blessed them and handed them to Joe and Sam to place on one another. Then they said, "I do," and walked down the aisle as husband and wife. Erica ran over to me and we took some pictures in the orange-dusk of the setting sun, the perfect light for wedding photos, before she asked me, "Are you happy, babe?"

"Yeah. Yeah, I am."

Then everybody headed to the reception hall for cocktail hour and speeches. My toast centered around the hilarious first encounter between Joe and Sam when she shut him down hard. Yet, here they were a few years later marrying each other. Funny how life always finds a way to put the right people together. Anyway, I ended the speech by talking about the unselfish love between Joe and Sam, and how we should all seek to emulate that kind of love. It was a feel-good toast, and Joe and Sam each gave me a hug when I was done.

As I sat down to listen to the maid of honor's speech, I looked around the room to see everyone with content smiles on their faces. No one was thinking of their everyday problems, the grind of work, or the fears that haunted them. They very likely thought of the best days of their lives as they shared in building one of the best days of Joe and Sam's lives. This is what it's all about; building these moments together is the purpose of life. And in that moment, it dawned on me how close I was to not being there. I felt the weight of my own loss realizing that my empty chair would've been like an arrow piercing the hearts of those who loved me. Right then and there, I promised myself no matter what the future held, I'd always find a way to choose life.

After dinner, the alcohol flowed, the men loosened their ties, and the women kicked off their heels. It was turn up time. The dance floor filled with guests letting loose and celebrating while Joe and Sam beamed with joy at the center of it all. "I Gotta Feeling" by the Black-Eyed Peas played, and my Dad pointed at Joe and I with two thumbs-up the way he always did when we heard that song after our first trip to Penn State together. As I gave the thumbs-up back, I thought of all that had happened since the day I stood at the edge of Beaver Stadium. All the pain, anger, confusion, brokenness, despair – all of it left me that night. I forgave myself for wanting to take my own life and set myself free from the prison of depression.

As Erica and I danced together, memories from my life flicked through my mind's eye, each experience contributing to the whole of who I was. Sledding on a snow-covered hill, my Mom's blonde hair poking out of her black cap. Holding onto Gabriel as a look of pure joy came over his face while we rode the Rubber Ducky ride at Sesame Street. Coffee coming out of my Dad's nose when we played *Tanks* for the Wii and he blew himself up by accident. My Mom-Mom, who hated all things sour, making a face of disgust when Joe and I tricked her into drinking lemon juice. My Pop-Pop performing his ritualistic bouncing at the knees before throwing his bowling ball down the lane. Erica and I ice-skating in Bryant Park. My Nan and I standing on the balcony of her apartment watching the sunset and her telling me she thinks everything matters. All these memories wove together to paint a picture of purpose and hope showing me one, eternal truth; Life is always worth living.

The memories rushed forward becoming images from a life I hadn't lived yet; visions of a future waiting eagerly for me. Erica and I were married hurrying about with young kids in a movie-like scene on Thanksgiving at my parents. Joe and Sam were over too with their middle schoolers and golden retriever, Kai. It was cold, so my Dad started a fire in the fire pit out back. His hair was grayer, and he moved stiffly as if his joints needed to be oiled, but he looked content. My Mom hummed Christmas songs to herself as she checked the turkey, smiling as Joe and I took Gabriel and the kids out to play football in keeping with holiday tradition.

Then, the scene dissolved showing Erica and I on a beach. There was the rhythmic sound of the ocean, the smell of the salt air, and the gentle rustling of the grass dunes. We strolled along the soft part of the shore not saying anything, our fingers inter-twined.

The beach scene melted into one of us in a snowy field. Oak-scented smoke rose from a nearby chimney. Fluffy, grey clouds hung low in the sky promising more snow to come.

A burst of color washed away the blanket of white to show Erica and I standing together in my childhood backyard at the height of fall. Leaves decorated the surrounding trees in bright golds, rich oranges, and deep reds. The scent of hay and pump-kin seeds floated by on a chill breeze. Our kids played in the yard with our three dogs (a chocolate lab, golden retriever, and boston terrier). Joe and Sam were there with their children too. Joe stood with his hands in his pockets; Sam looped her arm through the bend of his elbow and rested her head against his shoulder. Gabriel sat on the swing petting the lab while our kids played with him. He was, as always, thrilled to be the center of attention. My parents rested on a nearby bench, soft smiles stretched across their wrinkled faces.

Future-me had the same trimmed beard I have today. The last of his blonde hair was gone, traded in for a mature brown. His dark eyes were warm and knowing. He had light bags under his eyes which gave him a look of experience rather than one of exhaustion. On his finger was a simple wedding band. Everything about him was simple and solid; the picture of a man at peace.

This is all the life I have left to live.

This is the other side.

This is what waits for you, for all of us, on the other side of depression; a beautiful, fulfilling life we deserve. There is always hope. There is always a choice. There is always the goodness of life.

I've got all this life left to live.

You've got all this life left to live too.

Where Am I Now

As I wrote this book and sought ways to share my story of hope, I stumbled across a wonderful organization called Minding Your Mind. They are a non-profit organization dedicated to preventing mental health crises through education. Their main program centers around young adult speakers like myself telling our stories of recovery and sharing our insights for living a full life, despite our struggles with mental health. Minding Your Mind also offers programs for parents, teachers, workplaces, and community organizations. You can check out all that they have to offer (and donate if you're so inclined) at mindingyourmind.org.

Towards the end of my presentation, I always tell the audience that I'm not afraid of the future anymore; I'm excited for it. For so long in my life, I couldn't see a future, but now I can, and the future I envisioned in my last story is becoming a reality. At the time of this writing, Erica and I are only a month away from our wedding, and despite all we have had to contend with, we both feel incredibly blessed. We share an apartment together in New Jersey and find joy in the little things. We don't have any kids or dogs yet, but, God-willing, we'll have both in time.

How You Can Help

First and foremost, be kind to yourself. Take time to learn what's important to you, and why it's important to you. Deeply understanding who we are grounds us and gives us a direction to aim.

Second, if you found this book hopeful, please share it with those around you. You may unknowingly help someone in need. You can also visit amazon.com and leave an honest review about your thoughts on this book. What you have to say may convince someone who is struggling to read it. You have the potential to help them heal – nothing is as powerful as authentic testimony! Thank you!

Acknowledgements

There are so many people to thank, it's hard to know where to begin, so I guess I'll start with the people who brought me into this world. Mom, thank you for your tender compassion and gentle wisdom. You gave me the courage to persevere when I was broken. Dad, thank you for your unflinching moral clarity, which helped me to see life is always worth living. My strength comes from you, and it is with that strength that I was able to bear the pain of depression.

Thank you to Erica, my wonderful wife. You have given peace to my wild and restless heart. I would be lost without you.

Joe, thank you for sticking with me all these years, especially the years I was a jackass. Your friendship and twinship means the world to me. Thank you also for all the work you did editing and proofreading this book – it would not be what it is without your help.

Gabriel, thank you for all you have taught me about life. Your simple joy has shown me that there is purpose in even the most painful of circumstances.

Orto, thank you for your friendship and for your humble, yet profound editing insights. A great deal of the clarity within this book can be attributed to your thoughtfulness.

Diane and Elizabeth, thank you both for speaking to me with compassion and authenticity during the lowest time of my life. Your heartfelt empathy gave me hope when I had none, and I pray that this book does for others, what you have done for me.

Mr. Danilak, you took a chance on me when you allowed me to speak to the students of Holy Ghost about my battle with depression, and that has served as the launching point for my passion in helping others reach the other side of their mental health battle. Thank you for blessing me with this opportunity.

Dr. Aaron Pollock, thank you for meeting with me and taking the time to listen. You guided me towards Minding Your Mind, and I will be forever grateful.

To all those who work at Minding Your Mind, thank you for building such a wonderful, life-changing organization, and thank you further for allowing me to share in that. You know what it takes to build joy in this world.

Last but not least, thank you John. Your warmth, compassion, and quackiness brought me back from the brink of destruction. You have given me a second chance at life; a fuller, richer, more beautiful life. From the bottom of my heart, thank you.

About the Author

Lucas Wolfe has been writing and speaking publicly as a mental health advocate for over three years now. He has spoken to thousands of people about his struggle with depression and suicide and how he ultimately found purpose through his pain. His writing has been featured in articles with CNN affiliates, and on the blog *Beyond the Interview*. He has written articles for *The Mighty* as well as *Medium*. Lucas currently lives in New Jersey with his wife, Erica. You can keep up with all he is doing to inspire hope at his website – Lucasawolfe.com - or email him directly at Lucas@Lucasawolfe.com

Notes

Sophomore Year: Failure and Change

10. CancerianSoul. (2011, January 16). Good Will Hunting - "What Do You Wanna Do?" Retrieved from https://www.youtube.com/watch?v=zKQBHkzOYvw

13. Maya Angelou. (2019, November 7). Retrieved from https://achievement.org/achiever/maya-angelou/#interview

22. The Road Not Taken by Robert Frost. (2020). Retrieved from https://www.poetryfoundation.org/poems/44272/the-road-not-taken

Junior Year: Slipping Away

41. Movieclips. (2011, June 27). Happy Gilmore (9/9) Movie CLIP - Happy's Short Game (1996) HD. Retrieved from https://www.youtube.com/watch?v=7BwxSHs9elk

Senior Year: The Breaking Point

55. Gisele Mogilevich. (2009, May 11). Jack and Desmond. Retrieved from https://www.youtube.com/watch?v=AHmKKARwfYQ

77. The Mag: Penn runner's depression masked on social media. (2015, May 7). Retrieved from http://www.espn. com/espn/feature/story/_/id/12833146/instagram-account-university-pennsylvania-runner-showed-only-part-story

New Mexico: How My Greatest Victory Tortured Me

119. Understanding the Symptoms of Depression. (2002, November 1). Retrieved from https://www.webmd.com/ depression/understanding-depression-symptoms

Choices: Get Help or Die

127. xezene1. (2011, February 21). Harry Potter - "Light and Darkness." Retrieved from https://www.youtube.com /watch?v=hxDLoeDTXl0

131. The Mag: Penn runner's depression masked on social media. (2015, May 7). Retrieved from http://www.espn.com/espn/feature/story/_/id/12833146 /instagram-account-university-pennsylvania-runner-showed-only-part-story

Recovery: How Reaching Out Saved My Life

150. Motivation Ready. (2018, January 14). Motivation Ready - Four Minute Barrier ft. Les Brown (Roger Bannister). Retrieved from https://www.youtube.com/watch?v=w9PUafcJLvU

After: All This Life Left To Live

194. Gordon Logsdon. (2017, April 26). Shrek Welcome To Duloc. Retrieved from https://www.youtube.com/watch?v=LUHGyZQHp8I

195. Skill Hikes. (2015, September 10). Kung Fu Panda The Secret Ingredient. Retrieved from https://www.youtube.com/watch?v=MiE4UI5mfaA

201. Wokeness Drives Latino Student To Trump. (2019, November 13). Retrieved from https://www.theamericanconservative.com/dreher/wokeness-drives-latino-libertarian-to-trump/

202. CancerianSoul. (2011, January 16). Good Will Hunting - "What Do You Wanna Do?" Retrieved from https://www.youtube.com/watch?v=zKQBHkzOYvw

203. Miramax. (2015, December 15). Good Will Hunting | 'The Best Part of My Day' (HD) - Ben Affleck, Matt Damon | MIRAMAX. Retrieved from https://www.youtube.com/watch?v=Xv7eeMikM_w

210. Guardians of the Galaxy | Transcripts Wiki | Fandom. (2014, August 1). Retrieved from https://transcripts .fandom.com/wiki/Guardians_of_the_Galaxy

210. Pain In The Nation. (2019, June 1). Retrieved from http://www.paininthenation.org/

220. Is religion the opium of the people? | The question. (2017, May 8). Retrieved from https://www.theguardian.com/commentisfree/belief/2009/jun/26/religion-philosophy

Made in USA - Kendallville, IN
1164210_9798673886076
12.18.2020 1254